HISTORY MATTERS

HISTORY MATTERS

Teaching and learning history in New Zealand
secondary schools in the 21st century

MICHAEL HARCOURT
AND MARK SHEEHAN (EDITORS)

NZCER PRESS

2012

NZCER Press
New Zealand Council for Educational Research
PO Box 3237, Wellington, New Zealand

© 2012 Authors

National Library of New Zealand Cataloguing-in-Publication Data
History matters : teaching and learning history in New Zealand secondary schools in the 21st century / Michael Harcourt and Mark Sheehan, editors.
Includes bibliographical references.
ISBN 978-1-927151-56-3

1. History—Study and teaching (Secondary)—New Zealand.
I. Harcourt, Michael. II. Sheehan, Mark. III. New Zealand Council for Educational Research.
907.1293—dc 23

All rights reserved

Designed by Lynn Peck, Central Media
Printed by Pinnacle Print, Wellington

This title is also available as an e-book
from www.nzcer.org.nz/nzcerpress

Distributed by NZCER
PO Box 3237
Wellington
New Zealand
www.nzcer.org.nz

CONTENTS

Foreword **CHRISTINE COUNSELL** 1

Introduction **MICHAEL HARCOURT** and **MARK SHEEHAN** 5

Chapter 1: Teaching historical empathy and the 1915 Gallipoli campaign **MARTYN DAVISON** 11

Chapter 2: Pictorial pedagogies: Interpreting historical images as evidence **BARBARA ORMOND** 33

Chapter 3: Have you asked your students? Pasifika perspectives on studying history **CHRISTINA REYMER** 57

Chapter 4: Museums and historical literacy: Unpacking the narratives of war and nationhood **BRONWYN HOULISTON** 73

Chapter 5: Kua takoto te mānuka: The challenge of contested histories **PAUL ENRIGHT** 85

Chapter 6: Learning to think historically: Developing historical thinking through internally assessed research projects **MARK SHEEHAN and JONATHAN HOWSON** 105

Chapter 7: Facebook and teaching history **LARA HEARN-ROLLO** 117

Chapter 8: Contestable views and voices: If only history involved time travel! **CHARLOTTE McNAMARA** 127

Chapter 9: Where to next? Some final thoughts on the future of history teaching in New Zealand **MICHAEL HARCOURT** 141

Opening Speech New Zealand History Teachers' Association Conference 2010 **DR PITA SHARPLES** 149

Acknowledgements

The editors are grateful for the financial support from the New Zealand History Teachers' Association that allowed us to run a writing workshop for the authors in Wellington in August 2011, and to Christine Counsell (Cambridge University Faculty of Education) for writing the foreword.

FOREWORD

In July 2011, I greatly enjoyed working with the New Zealand history education community at the Social Sciences Conference, *SocCon 2011*, in Wellington. This was my kind of conference: teachers in the vast majority, academics—all of whom had been teachers and still worked in schools—and educators from many other settings. Knowledge was constructed through scholarly conversations about the 'what', 'how' and 'why' of teaching each discipline.

Every teacher at that conference was a scholar, because each was doing what scholars do: turning challenging problems into good questions, exploring ways of solving those problems with others, submitting their own ideas for intellectual, practical or ethical scrutiny, situating their practice within other discourses, explaining the warrant—moral, empirical or theoretical—for their own ideas. Such a conference is a dynamic, living canon—it takes bearings from the existing canon of history educators' professional and scholarly knowledge, it gives that knowledge new expression, and it renews itself, so that collective knowledge about education becomes a conversation between past and present.

For history educators, there are a small but growing number of such conferences throughout the world. Their characteristics are enthusiasm and energy, a sense of collective professional agency, a scholarly responsibility for shaping future curricula and pedagogy. At these conferences, teacher identity and scholar identity fold into one. These are history teachers passionate about defining, developing and declaring 'high standards' agendas for themselves. To attend them, history teachers will even give up their own time and find their own funds. As an academic, I prize them above all other conferences: these are the places where tough intellectual problems are addressed, where new knowledge—sometimes brilliantly innovative and theoretically powerful—is made, and where one's original teacher identity and teacher knowledge can surface and find new kinds of challenge.

All too often, scholarly books do not do what the great history education conferences do. Apart from a couple of token chapters, a strange, vicarious discourse is enacted, as though teachers needed someone to speak on their behalf. The questions, debates and research about history education are advanced chiefly by university academics, with teachers' voices present only as the object of enquiry—as research subjects, as statistics, as perspectives to be quoted or analysed.

This points to the first reason why this book is so important. Its authors construct knowledge in many ways—through systematic empirical enquiry, through reflection on the meaning and experience of practice, through comparative analysis across contrasting discourses, through adaptation of others' theories and theorising of their own, but each chapter is infused with a particular quality of insight that comes from being or having been a classroom teacher in a particular subject community. It is the lens of the problem-solving history teacher that is peculiarly generative of this rich scholarship and that shapes teachers' agency as curriculum theorists.

Curricular theorising links to the second reason for my enthusiasm for this book. Each author problematizes the 'What?' of history education as much as the 'How?'. By 'What?', I do not mean content choice; I mean the quest to define the discipline of history itself and to give it curricular expression. Each is asking, what *kind* of powerful thinking does the practice of history distinctively provide? The authors thus bear out Elliott's (1993) claim that criticality inheres in teachers' practical enquiry. Whatever the authors' pedagogic concerns—the inclusion of marginalized students, the value of internal assessment, and the potential of Facebook—the discussion is ultimately one of how a history teacher is to operate consistently within an intellectual framework that has transparent rigour, a framework that empowers and emancipates. What should be the characteristics of that framework? How should we promote and reward progression within it? To ask how students might become participants in a disciplinary conversation about history is to ask what are the properties of that conversation, who constructs it, what is it for and under what conditions can it be held.

These issues burn the world over; none are peculiar to New Zealand. But the authors avoid the usual, wearisome oscillation between two redundant poles. At one pole, national governments try to build social cohesion by engaging in a futile quest to establish or re-establish one official narrative. In Lebanon, there are riots over the latest failed effort to write a history textbook that will unite. In England, still no new curriculum emerges, and the government now appears paralysed by the practical impossibility of imposing a single narrative. The effort to reduce school history to one story can only fail. At the other pole, where disciplinary knowledge is deemed alienating, we see curricula collapsing into a mere mirroring of student experience, while generic, context-free 'information skills' or 'thinking skills' replace subject structures.

The latter approach cuts pupils off from the conceptual reference points and disciplined thinking that can give them power. In history, powerful forms of thinking require explicit teaching; they will not emerge from experience alone. The special condition of temporality—how human societies continuously shape meaning from their pasts, over time—demands special forms of enquiry. Pupils cannot judge the validity of an historical account if they do not understand how such accounts are constructed. They cannot emplot new narratives if they have not reflected on the nature of historical change, continuity and causation, understanding how each works differently in history from in (say) science. They will never be able to deconstruct the discourses around them—discourses replete with assumptions about the past and subtly pervasive in every commemorative act, every political slogan, every polemic, every social policy, every international posture—if they have no abstract concepts and no means for distinguishing between a relic *from* the past and its use in subsequent, constructed account.

Yet what is striking about this volume is the deep sensitivity, the ethic of care towards students and respect for their contexts, the culture of scholarly enquiry concerning ways of understanding student perspective.

None of this detracts from the concern to induct students into traditions of intellectual enquiry which, like all genuinely educative experiences, will challenge and disturb as much as they affirm and celebrate. For far from ignoring the powerful interests that may have constructed knowledge canons, the practice of the discipline of history, as conceived in this volume, constantly examines the motives, methods and claims that any constructed account of the past—museum, textbook, scholarly work or political act—will reveal and conceal. Criticality in this kind of school history involves uncovering the interests that constructed its own canon.

Nor are the authors in this volume complacent about this as a solution; rather they show that when we ask hard questions, such as whether the practice of that very criticality might be disruptive of traditional values, the results of listening to students might surprise us. Christina Reymer finds that the most complex features of historical knowledge—its constructed and contested character—can be understood through the lens of students' own cultural traditions. Such work connects powerfully with teachers elsewhere who are similarly exploring the relationship between disciplinary practices and student identity or motivation (Whitburn and Yemoh 2012; Baker and Mastin 2012). This volume demonstrates amply that the continuing effort to define such disciplinary practice is the proper work of history teachers.

Christine Counsell
University of Cambridge, August 2012

References

Baker, B. and Mastin, S. (2012) Did Alexander really ask, 'Do I appear to you to be a bastard?' Using ancient texts to improve pupils' critical thinking. *Teaching History*, *147*.

Elliott, J. (1993) The relationship between understanding and developing teachers' thinking. In J. Elliott (ed.) *Reconstructing Teacher Education: Teacher development*. London: The Falmer Press

Whitburn, R. and Yemoh, S. (2012) 'My people struggled too': hidden histories and heroism—a school-designed, post-14 course on multi-cultural Britain since 1945. *Teaching History*, *147*.

INTRODUCTION

Michael Harcourt and Mark Sheehan

This is an exciting time to be teaching senior history in New Zealand. Recent developments in *The New Zealand Curriculum* and the alignment of the *Curriculum* with the Achievement Standards now offer ongoing opportunities for history teachers and students to engage with increasingly innovative approaches to understanding the past that reflect historical thinking. In the *Curriculum* senior secondary school history students are now expected to engage with the disciplinary features of the subject (such as argument, evidence, significance and interpretation) to a much greater extent than previously.

This book reflects the dynamic and changing nature of teaching and learning history in New Zealand secondary classrooms and the growing maturity of the history teaching community. It aims to contribute to ongoing conversations over questions such as:

- Why do we teach history?
- How do students learn to do history?
- What motivates history students?
- What does history have to offer adolescents in the 21st century?
- How can we incorporate an authentic Māori and Pasifika dimension into our history programmes?

In tackling such questions, the aim is to bridge the gap between theory and practice among secondary history teachers and to draw on the wealth of talent, enthusiasm and expertise within the history teaching community.

MICHAEL HARCOURT and MARK SHEEHAN

The idea for the book came out of the New Zealand History Teachers' Association (NZHTA) conference in Wellington in October 2010. Attended by almost 150 teachers, it was a conference that saw a number of papers, workshops and keynotes that addressed the opportunities and challenges of teaching and learning history. This included the opening speech from the then Associate Minister of Education, Dr Pita Sharples (reprinted in this book), which challenged the history teaching community to reflect on the "selective portrayal of New Zealand history" in the past, and a panel of researchers from the Institute of Education in London, who discussed what thinking historically might mean for New Zealand in the 21st century.

The concerns faced by the history teaching community in New Zealand are far from straightforward. They defy simple answers and require carefully considered responses that are informed by research. This book does not claim to provide all the answers, but it is a contribution to the sorts of conversations that history teachers are currently engaging in to improve our understanding of what it means to teach history in New Zealand in the second decade of the 21st century.

The authors are a diverse group. They were selected by the editors after an open invitation for expressions of interest was sent out in April 2011 to the history teaching community via the NZHTA website, regional subject association websites, and university faculties of education and history departments. Reflecting the current student demographic, five authors are from Auckland, two from Dunedin and two from Wellington. Some of the authors are at the beginning of their careers, while others have been part of the history teaching community for many years and have been closely involved with national and regional subject associations and Ministry of Education and New Zealand Qualifications Authority initiatives. All of the chapters were peer reviewed.

As editors it was an enormous privilege to work with these teacher writers and researchers. Not only do all share a passion for secondary school history and a steadfast determination to ensure that the subject continues to be based on the key features of historical thinking, but all are either practising classroom history teachers or have been in the classroom relatively recently. In this we see a growing appreciation within the history teaching community of the value of research-informed practice, as well as a commitment to developing a research literature on teaching and learning history in New Zealand that is for teachers and by teachers.

To this end, the book provides a platform for teachers' voice with regard to teaching and learning history that, while not playing down the challenges, reflects innovative initiatives in classroom practice in this subject community. The editors appreciated the enthusiasm of the authors for the project, their commitment to shifting thinking about teaching and learning history, and their courage to share their insights about historical thinking in all its different forms with their colleagues in the history teaching community.

Martyn Davison in Chapter 1 explores the concept of historical empathy in a New Zealand context (namely, the Gallipoli campaign). The process of engaging in historical empathy is both cognitive (thinking) and affective (feeling). It is cognitive because it requires thinking about how pieces of evidence fit together; it is affective because it attempts to imagine what an historical character might have felt. In this chapter the author outlines a sequence of learning activities that engage with historical empathy's cognitive and affective dimensions and describes the challenges students face when they participate in this type of learning. He also explores the assessment of historical empathy and the different ways of thinking about how to plan for student progression.

Barbara Ormond in Chapter 2 explores how the visual culture of peoples of the past provides a unique perspective on societies as they were seen through the eyes of artists, illustrators and publishers. Pictorial evidence, she argues, can support, contradict or nuance understanding gained through other forms of evidence, and can reveal ideas that may not be stated explicitly in text. It is also recognised in the key competencies in the *Curriculum* and is a key element of historical thinking, as when students engage in interpreting unfamiliar visual evidence from the past and are required to contextualise it through reference to multiple sources. In light of these factors, there is a need for more robust pedagogies to help students acquire the tools to interpret images in relation to the representational modes of a particular time and place.

Christina Reymer in Chapter 3 considers how Pasifika students' identities affect how they experience history. She argues that the cultural and religious understanding that many Pasifika students have of the past and their personal connections with history have important implications for history teachers. This is especially important for how these students engage with the interpretive and contested features of the subject, and Christina observes that when she worked within a culturally appropriate framework, Pasifika students were more comfortable contesting historical claims. Her chapter challenges teachers to make a conscious effort to avoid the deficit theorising that occurs in relation to Pasifika students, and to recognise that these students are able to understand the complex nature of historical knowledge through the lens of their own cultural understanding. She also found that, despite some historical content not being explicitly relevant to them, Pasifika students were able to make personal connections with the past by drawing comparisons between the cultural traditions of other societies (both past and present) and their own.

Bronwyn Houliston in Chapter 4 uses the permanent exhibition of New Zealand's war experience at Auckland War Memorial Museum, *Scars on the Heart*, to examine how history students can be taught to look beyond the label and recognise areas of contention and contestability when they encounter museum exhibits that set out to tell a dominant narrative of national identity. Such exhibits seldom reflect the interpretive nature of the discipline, and, drawing on examples of New Zealand's military experience, she considers how dissenting viewpoints are overwhelmingly marginalised in the exhibit in favour of narrative that emphasises the seamless development of a unified nation. She suggests a number of approaches to encourage students to develop the tools of historical thinking to engage with the contested nature of museum exhibits so that they open up a dialogue about the past, rather than passively accepting fixed historical truths.

Paul Enright in Chapter 5 makes the case that all history is contested and argues that those teaching approaches that reflect this view are able to anchor school history more firmly in the essential disciplines of the parent subject and develop historical thinking among students. Making explicit links to the realigned Level 3 standards that embed a perspectives strand through NCEA Levels 1, 2 and 3, the author advocates taking a pragmatic pedagogical approach to initial programmes, building on current practices as teachers test and develop strategies to assist students' progression through and within the curriculum levels.

Mark Sheehan and **Jonathan Howson** in Chapter 6 discuss the initial findings of a Teaching and Learning Research Initiative (TLRI) study that is examining how senior secondary school history students are motivated to develop expertise in the disciplinary features of the subject through internally assessed research projects. It appears that not only does this style of learning generate high levels of intrinsic motivation among students, but that engaging with the processes of how knowledge is produced in the discipline through research projects contributes to students developing high levels of disciplinary expertise.

Lara Hearn-Rollo in Chapter 7 explores how we incorporate online technologies into history programmes, and in particular the place of Facebook in maintaining a community of learners in the subject and as a teaching tool that fosters historical thinking. She outlines how she has used the medium to provide an open forum for teachers and students to discuss their ideas, their research and new paths down which to pursue their current line of thinking, particularly for internal assessments. She also draws on Sam Wineburg's work to consider how Facebook can help with key features of historical thinking, such as sourcing, contextualising, close reading and corroborating.

Charlotte McNamara in Chapter 8 explores how she shifted her thinking about teaching and learning history from first-order concepts, such as key personalities and events, to second-order historical concepts, such as causation and significance. She found that when she conveyed this insight to her students, it enabled them to see their learning of history as a *process* of understanding people of the past through the lens of historical agency. She argues that grasping historical agency involves students developing an understanding that people in the past are a product of their times. As history teachers we need to provide opportunities for our students to gain insight and understanding of historical events through individual, collective and institutional historical agency, and the subsequent outcomes of this agency in terms of whether or not situations stayed the same or changed.

In chapter 9 **Michael Harcourt** considers the challenges and opportunities of teaching history in the 21st century especially in light of the changing social and cultural features of New Zealand society. The book concludes with the opening speech from the then Associate Minister of Education, Dr Pita Sharples that lays down a challenge to the history teaching community to address the "selective portrayal of New Zealand history" in the past.

CHAPTER 1

Teaching historical empathy and the 1915 Gallipoli campaign

MARTYN DAVISON

Martyn Davison has been a secondary school teacher since 1996. He began teaching in Plymouth, England, and took the plunge to these Pacific shores in 2002. He has a particular interest in practitioner inquiry and how teachers can contribute to the field of educational research. Martyn is currently enrolled part-time in the Doctor of Education programme at The University of Auckland. His doctoral thesis explores how a small group of students at a large suburban secondary school developed a sophisticated grasp of historical empathy.

Martyn can be contacted at: mdav120@aucklanduni.ac.nz

Introduction

This chapter explores the concept of historical empathy and how it can foster a greater understanding of a significant episode in New Zealand and Australian history, the 1915 Gallipoli campaign.[1] In doing so, it draws upon my experience of teaching historical empathy to Year 10/11 (14-

---

[1] The Gallipoli campaign in 1915 is sometimes described as a side-show in the larger history of the First World War. For the Australian and New Zealand Army Corps (ANZAC) it was a defeat which foreshadowed worse losses on the Western Front. However, 8,709 Australians and 2,721 New Zealanders lost their lives in the campaign, and as a place where the ANZAC spirit was forged it has found a significant place in the narrative of New Zealand and Australian history.

to 16-year-old) students and from trying to make sense of the extensive literature on the concept.

The chapter is divided into three sections. I begin by defining historical empathy and justifying why it is worthwhile pursuing in the classroom. The second section outlines a sequence of learning activities that deliberately engage with historical empathy's cognitive (thinking) and affective (feeling) dimensions. It also briefly describes the problems and successes I experienced as students engaged with these activities. The final section explores the assessment of historical empathy and the different ways of thinking about how to plan for student progression. It makes the case for trying to exemplify what being good at historical empathy looks like.

What is historical empathy?

Historical empathy is often thought of as vicariously walking in someone else's shoes in order to interpret how that person feels about things, and to understand why they might have travelled down one road and not another. As a definition this is a good start, but it doesn't tell us much about exactly how we go about stepping into the shoes of an historical character.

According to historian John Lewis Gaddis, the way to do this is to begin by "getting inside other people's minds … [by allowing your own mind to] be open to their impressions—their hopes and fears, their beliefs and dreams" (2002, p. 124). This sometimes requires temporarily taking seriously views that might seem strangely different to our own. This doesn't mean having to agree or identify with these views. As the philosopher M.L. Hoffman makes clear, "empathy doesn't deprive the empathetic individual of her sense of being a different person from the person she empathises with" (2000, p. 14). In other words, historical empathy does not remove the ability to think critically about an historical character's beliefs. This is because once an empathetic person has taken in the views of an historical character they, to use Gaddis's phrase, "bail out" and then begin to critically make sense of what they have experienced.

This process of historical empathy is both cognitive and affective. It is cognitive because it requires thinking about how pieces of evidence fit together. It is affective because it attempts to imagine what an historical character might have felt. Based on the different ways in which various researchers—notably Lee (1984), Shemilt (1984), Downey (1996), Foster (2001), Dulberg (2002), and Barton and Levstik (2004)—think about historical empathy, I have outlined in Table 1.1 what these cognitive and affective dimensions might look like.

Table 1.1. The cognitive and affective dimensions of historical empathy

Cognitive (thinking)	Affective (feeling)
Building historical contextual knowledge	Using imagination to recognise appropriate feelings
Being aware of the past as being different from the present	Listening to and entertaining other points of view
Tying interpretations of the past to evidence	Being caring, sensitive and tolerant towards other people

This outline helps to de-mystify the meaning of historical empathy, something that may be helpful to teachers because the wider literature abounds with definitions (Brooks, 2009). Put simply, through open-minded observation and paying attention we can come to know something of others. When we do this for people who lived in the past, this mindfulness is based on what the historian J.H. Hexter (1971) called the "record of the past", which is often referred to as historical evidence.

Having established that historical empathy requires students to enter into the past, but also to remain somewhat aloof from it, and to work both cognitively and affectively, it can be defined as:

> Enter[ing] into some informed appreciation of the predicaments or points of view of other people in the past ... it is simply a word used to describe the imagination working on evidence, attempting to enter into a past experience while at the same time remaining outside it. (Department of Education and Science [UK], 1985, p. 3)

Why teach historical empathy? In the last 30 years it has sometimes been more tempting to think about the reasons why *not* to teach historical empathy. This is because it has often been associated with sympathy, unrestrained imagination and over-identification, leading to the claim that it produces a 'let's pretend' version of history. The counterargument is to see historical empathy as a key component of what is meant by doing history, and to link it with the wider goal of developing the civic values of students.

Historical empathy is frequently included in various models that attempt to describe how history can be taught as a school subject (Seixas & Peck, 2004; Taylor, 2011; Van Drie & Van Boxtel, 2008). In these models, historical empathy is variously described as a crucial element of historical thinking (Seixas & Peck, 2004), what it means to be historically literate (Taylor, 2011), and as a meta-concept which helps to form a framework of historical reasoning (Van Drie & Van Boxtel, 2008). In other words, those who advocate the teaching of historical thinking invariably include historical empathy within a framework of how that should be envisioned. As Table 1.1 helps to make clear, historical empathy encompasses attributes and skills closely associated with doing history. Teaching historical empathy, however, is potentially more than simply mirroring the practices of professional historians. It might also be taught to serve the common good, as proposed by Barton and Levstik (2004).

The idea of empathy serving the common good comes largely from the perspective of psychotherapy (McWilliams, 2004) and moral philosophy (Hoffman, 2000; Slote, 2007, 2010), where it is seen as a mechanism for helping people. Empathy is placed at the heart of civic society by Hoffman when he argues that it is "the spark of human concern for others, the glue that makes social life possible" (2000, p. 3), and by Slote when he posits that empathy is a "mechanism of caring, benevolence, compassion" (2007, p. 4). Meier (1996) is no less emphatic, arguing that the informed scepticism of democratic societies is nurtured through empathy. She suggests that as citizens we develop

> the habit of stepping into the shoes of others—both intellectually and emotionally. We need literally to be able to experience, if even for a very short time, the ideas, feelings, pains, and mind-sets of others, even when doing so creates some discomfort. (1996, p. 272)

My rationale for teaching historical empathy, therefore, rests on the idea that it enables students to understand the lives of others, past and present, by affectively tuning in to shared human traits and by cognitively comprehending why another person holds a different set of beliefs. This position is reflected in the aims of *The New Zealand Curriculum* (Ministry of Education, 2007). Firstly, historical empathy can be linked to the *Curriculum*'s key competency *relating to others*, in so far as it focuses on students' "ability to listen actively, recognise different points of view, negotiate, and share ideas" (p. 12). Secondly, the *Curriculum* is relevant to historical empathy because it states that a goal of the Social Sciences learning area is to explore how "people ... are shaped by perspectives [and how] others see themselves" (p. 30). The *Curriculum* achievement objectives for history also emphasise interpreting people's perspectives.

Teaching historical empathy

My teaching of historical empathy and Gallipoli takes place across 18 one-hour lessons. It is guided by two historical questions: "In 1914/15, why did so many young men decide to leave New Zealand and Australia and travel half way around the world to fight in a war?" and "What was it like fighting on the Gallipoli peninsula in 1915?" These questions are intended to be genuinely puzzling, although this intention might be undone by the students' prior knowledge of Gallipoli. It is a good idea, then, to gauge students' prior knowledge through something like a source-based pre-task. The results will probably influence teacher decisions about the degree of challenge involved in subsequent learning activities. This exploring of prior knowledge also often provides an opportunity to make connections with students' own lives and thereby foster engagement (Donovan & Bransford, 2005). For instance, when I was completing these steps in 2010, students were interested in why New Zealand soldiers were serving in Afghanistan.

To fit around the inquiry's two historical questions, I devised a sequence of affective and cognitive learning activities (outlined below in Boxes 1 and 2). I started my teaching with the affective learning activities and then moved on to the cognitive because I believe this particular sequence has the potential to best promote student interest and enjoyment. However, this is contestable. As Dulberg (2002) points out, teachers can move back and forth between the affective and cognitive, or they can decide to focus more heavily on the cognitive, as Foster (2001) advocates. The crucial point is that teaching time is devoted to both the affective and cognitive.

> **Box 1: Affective learning activities**
>
> Learning activity 1: Watching the film *Gallipoli* (affective)
>
> This learning activity involves scaffolding the students' watching of Peter Weir's 1981 film *Gallipoli*. It aims to encourage listening to different viewpoints, caring about the film's characters, and helping students enter into the 1915 era.

Figure 1.1. Mark Lee (Archy) and Mel Gibson (Frank) standing together in *Gallipoli* (1981).
Director: Peter Weir, National Film and Sound Archive (Australia), title no: 357192.
Reproduced by kind permission of Associated R & R Films Pty Ltd.

The students are asked to identify the different perspectives of the following characters: Archy and his uncle, Frank and his mates, and Frank's father. It is pointed out that the music used as the men come ashore on the beaches of Gallipoli is Tomaso Giovanni Albinoni's *Adagio for Organ and Strings*. Students record their feelings when this music is being played. At the end of the film I use an extract from an interview with Peter Weir, Mel Gibson (Frank) and Mark Lee (Archy), which is included as a special feature on my DVD version of the film. Weir talks about how young men in 1914 had seen the war as an opportunity for change and adventure. Lee and Gibson talk about meeting Gallipoli veterans.

Learning activity 2: The local war memorial (affective)

Students are each given a copy of a name from a wax-crayon rubbing of the local war memorial. (Alternatively, the students can go to their own local war memorial and make the wax-crayon rubbing themselves.) The purpose of this learning activity is to engage the students with an individual soldier—someone they might begin to care about. The students use the Commonwealth War Graves Commission's website (http://www.cwgc.org/) to find out more about the soldier, including the details of their military record. The Auckland War Memorial Museum's website (http:/muse.aucklandmuseum.com/databases/cenotaph/locations.aspx) may also be useful. Next, students' select 50 words from the soldier's military record and reorder these to create a poem.

Learning activity 3: Picture response (affective)

Students explore their feelings about Gallipoli by responding to two sets of six A2-sized colour posters, published by Macmillan (Cormack, 2009). The posters are placed around the classroom for the students to visit in turn. A graphic organiser (adapted from Cormack's teacher notes) helps students to make their responses:

Gallipoli Today poster What would this area have looked like in 1915? Why do you think thousands of New Zealanders come to Gallipoli each year on Anzac Day?	*Map of the journey to Gallipoli poster* What does the map tell us about the distance between New Zealand and Gallipoli?
Life for the Anzacs poster What do these photographs tell you about life for soldiers and nurses?	*Dawn Service poster* How would an ex-soldier perhaps feel during the dawn service?
Anzac Battlefields poster Look at the photo of the cemetery. Describe the setting.	*Simpson and His Donkey poster* What emotions may Simpson have felt as he moved injured soldiers to safety?

Learning activity 4: Freeze-frames (affective)

This learning activity is adapted from material on the *facing history* website: http://www.facinghistory.org/resources/strategies/living-images-bringing-histor. It involves drawing the students closer to the events of 1915 by bringing to life what is portrayed in a series of photographs about Gallipoli.

Set A	Set B
1. Graduating nurses	1. Embarkation
2. Nurses on board ship	2. The rum issue
3. Wounded soldiers	3. Eve of an attack
4. Field hospital	4. Soldiers charging at the enemy
1, 3 and 4: Rees, 2008; 2: Donovan, 2005	1: Pugsley, 1984; 2, 3 and 4: Donovan, 2005

Figure 1.2. The rum issue.
Photographer attributed as Sydney Webb, image no: 29496, call number: album 338, p. 4. Reproduced by kind permission of the Auckland War Memorial Museum.

Students are given the choice of using photographs about the experience of nurses (Set A) or photographs focusing on soldiers (Set B). Working in groups, students re-enact the scenes in the photographs. The students therefore have to physically move into a role, which involves imagining the experiences of the characters in the photographs. Each group is asked to get into exactly the same position as the historical characters in the photograph and then hold this position, like a freeze-frame, for 10 seconds. The freeze-frames are presented to the rest of the class. Discussion follows about the feelings the activity has evoked.

Learning activity 5: Role-play (affective)

The aim of this learning activity is to use role-play to help students look at the particular experience of Bill Leadley, who was a signaller at Gallipoli (Chamberlain, 2008). Six of Bill's diary entries are selected. Each student is given two entries, for a particular month, and asked to learn some of the details before acting out the role of being Bill. Questions are asked of students and they answer these while in role; for example: How do you keep your spirits up? What is one of the most difficult things about being at Gallipoli? By answering these questions the students are acting out Bill's diary. There follows a discussion about what the students have learnt from Bill's diary and how Bill's impression of Gallipoli may have changed over time.

Box 2: Cognitive learning activities

Learning activity 1: Building historical context (cognitive)

I begin by looking at people's beliefs in 1914. I use TV One's 2005 documentary *Frontier of Dreams*, 'Episode 8: The price of empire' (Burke & Waru, 2005), to introduce the larger forces at play. I also use a mapping activity to look at the size of the British empire and its trading routes. Drawing on material from http://www.nzhistory.net.nz, I ask students to examine sources relating to: the Boy Scouts movement, military training, and HMS *New Zealand*'s visit to Wellington in 1913. The students also read relevant extracts from Michael King's *Penguin History of New Zealand* (King, 2003).

Learning activity 2: Historical newspapers (cognitive)

Groups of students are given a collection of short notices, advertisements or news articles from a 1915 copy of the *Waikato Times* newspaper. They are asked to record what they think the material says about the war. Next, they report back to the whole class and describe what they have recorded. I lead a discussion about the limitations and strengths of using newspapers as historical sources. I have been unable to find the origin of this resource, but pages from New Zealand newspapers of this era can be accessed online at: http://paperspast.natlib.govt.nz/cgi-bin/paperspast

Learning activity 3: The voices of veterans (cognitive)

The aim is to use the recollections of World War I veterans to explain why men went to war. Transcripts of veterans talking about Gallipoli are available online (http://www.abc.net.au/innovation/gallipoli/) or in print (Boyak & Tolerton, 1990; Cowan, 2011; Shadbolt, 1988). Working in pairs, the students are given a selection of transcripts to read, after which they draw up a table identifying the main reason why each veteran joined up. Once this is completed, students come up to the whiteboard and all of the results are collated. It quickly emerges which reasons are the most common. A whole-class discussion then takes place about the range of perspectives and what this activity might say about using evidence.

Learning activity 4: Building contextual knowledge of the landings (cognitive)

In this learning activity the students are encouraged to explore the wide range of online evidence that is available about Gallipoli. They access the Australian War Memorial website (http://www.abc.net.au/innovation/gallipoli/), which draws on a huge array of material containing multiple perspectives about what happened on the first day of the Gallipoli landings (25 April 1915). The students, working independently or in pairs, are asked to build up their knowledge of at least two different perspectives taken from the first day of landings.

Learning activity 5: Overcoming presentism (cognitive)

The aim is to explore the idea of the past being different from the present. The students watch the *ABC* documentary *Gallipoli: Brothers in Arms* (Denton, 2007), which follows a group of present-day Australians visiting Gallipoli. It also investigates what people in 1915 might have felt about Gallipoli and makes links between the past and present through the stories of two families. The students are given a graphic organiser to help them structure their note-taking:

	1915	The present day
Who was at Gallipoli?		
How do they feel about it?		
The physical terrain		
The dead		

Learning activity 6: Using evidence (cognitive)

The emphasis of this lesson is on tying the students' interpretations of Gallipoli to the evidence. Students are given a table of statistics and asked to respond to a single question: How do figures like this help us to understand Gallipoli and the meaning of Anzac? Next, they listen to historian Peter Pederson (Cessford, 2010) talking about conditions at Gallipoli, especially the food and drink. This helps students grasp that the Anzac diet of apricot jam, bully beef and biscuits was pretty wretched, and that dysentery was widespread.

> **Facts and figures**
> - The population of New Zealand in 1914 was just over 1 million.
> - 120,000 New Zealanders joined up.
> - 2,688 Māori and 346 Pacific Islanders served in a pioneer battalion.
> - 550 nurses served with the New Zealand Expeditionary Force and many others joined up in Britain.
> - 7,500 New Zealanders were wounded and 2,721 died at Gallipoli (that's one in four who landed), and 12,500 died in the following 2 years.
> - The names of the dead are recorded on 500 war memorials throughout New Zealand.
>
> Source: http://www.nzhistory.net.nz

Learning activity 7: Using evidence (cognitive)

This learning activity is about using a rubric to analyse a series of World War I cartoons. I model how a historian might approach these cartoons, using four questions:

- Where is the cartoon from?
- What can I see in the cartoon?
- What doesn't the cartoon tell me?
- What questions does the cartoon raise?

The students use these questions to analyse different cartoons. The National Library of New Zealand website (http://www.paperspast.natlib.govt.nz) is an excellent place to search for New Zealand cartoons of the First World War.

Figure 1.3. W. Blomfield [cartoonist]. (1915, 2 October). *The shirker—Is he to be the father of the future?* *New Zealand Observer*, XXXVI(4), 1. Reproduced by kind permission of the National Library of New Zealand.

Two problems emerged from these learning activities. Firstly, students rarely considered the provenance of sources. For instance, the provenance of Peter Weir's film *Gallipoli* was not questioned by the students. Despite the film's characters being fictional, their feelings were used by the students in the same way as the reflections of men who had actually served at Gallipoli in 1915. Admittedly I had used the film to help students imaginatively enter into the past, but I had hoped that by practising the cognitive dimension of historical empathy they would not have been so taken in, in the sense of uncritically accepting everything at face value. Alan Marcus's (2007) work on history and film may be useful here in terms of getting students to exercise greater caution in the context of watching films. As well as promoting film as an engaging re-creation of the past, Marcus explores how students can develop ways to critically interpret film.

A second problem was students not always contextualising the beliefs and actions of historical characters. This is perhaps not surprising, in so far as Wineburg's (2001, 2007) research has shown that even history undergraduates and history teachers find this difficult to do. This is because of the counterintuitive nature of historical thinking. The building of contextual knowledge takes a great deal of practice, and the strangeness of past contexts frequently means they are hard to make sense of from the perspective of the present. As Wineburg argues, our default setting is to rush in and make connections with the past rather than remain coolly detached from it. What is perhaps needed in the classroom is for history teachers to balance the aims of drawing students into the past, against explaining how they might comprehend what others have experienced by standing back and looking at events from another vantage point.

The successes that emanated from the learning activities included student enjoyment and interest in what they were doing, and many students developing a relatively sophisticated grasp of historical empathy. There is not the scope in this chapter to delve deeply into the reasons for these successes, but I would tentatively argue that they were based on engaging students in both the cognitive and the affective dimensions of historical empathy. I would also argue that by carefully planning a broad variety of learning activities, which allowed time for in-depth inquiry, and developing my own pedagogical knowledge of teaching historical empathy the outcomes for the students were enhanced.

Student progression and assessing historical empathy

At the end of the teaching sequence I assessed the students' grasp of historical empathy by asking them to write an essay focusing on the questions that had guided their inquiry. They were given two 1-hour periods to plan and write their essays. Lucy's[2] essay is reproduced here as an exemplar.

> Box 3: Lucy's essay about historical empathy and Gallipoli
>
> Why did a huge number of young men leave New Zealand in 1914/15 to fight a war thousands of kilometres away? And what were the effects of this decision upon these young men up until the end of 1915?
>
> In 1915, over 120,000 New Zealanders travelled by sea to Gallipoli, Turkey. They went to stand for their country, to see the world, to support their friends, and because they felt it was their duty. The result of this decision was not the glory that they had expected but the death of many young soldiers.
>
> The most common reason for soldiers to join the army was the hope of adventure. Most of the men settled in New Zealand during the time of the First World War had grown up on the isolated islands [New Zealand], and so the thought of adventure appealed to them. "It was more high adventure than anything else" (Vic Nicholson, ex-Anzac soldier). Soldiers felt it was their duty. Posters were put up which shunned the idea of not joining the army, calling those people "slackers".
>
> Eventually, most of those people who didn't think it as being their duty and thought it "wasn't their war" (Frank's character in the 1981 film *Gallipoli*) were blackmailed into either joining up or being sent to prison when the need came for more soldiers. "I joined up because it was my duty' (Russell Weir, ex-Anzac soldier). Joining the war was "the thing to do at the time" (Vic Nicolson). Soldiers also joined up because it was popular, and most of their friends were doing it. "I knew my mates would" (Joe Gasparich, ex-Anzac soldier). They also thought it would be fun to join up together.

---

2   Lucy is a Year 10 social studies student. A pseudonym has been used to ensure her anonymity.

The final, but not the only other reason, as it varies with different people, is because they were patriotic and loved their country: "We were very much for the British Empire. When the call came we went" (Bill East, ex-Anzac soldier). The soldiers wanted to fight for their country and its rights, believing they would return to New Zealand as heroes. "I don't think you could find a more patriotic volunteer than myself" (Joe Gasparich).

When the soldiers finally landed in Gallipoli after their long sea voyage, they found it was not as they expected. With gathered evidence from the diary of a young soldier, Bill Leadley, who was wounded at Gallipoli, we can understand the conditions that the soldiers were living in during the war. Bill Leadley describes the constant sound of war, the lack of hygiene, and the bad food and the dirty water. The heat was above thirty-five degrees Celsius and the men had bad sunburn. The heat was attracting flies, which added to the unhygienic conditions. Many of the soldiers were getting sick, and in June Leadley got dysentery, which got worse in September. He was also wounded in September, and states in his diary "I wish I could get well".

By the end of 1915 thousands of men had died, having lost their lives on the battlefield or from infected injuries and illnesses for which they didn't have the necessary medication to properly treat. When the Anzacs realised that there was no chance of possibly winning the battle against Turkey, with so many dead, they made a quick and successful evacuation. However, those lucky soldiers who had survived then travelled to the Western Front, located from the Belgian coast to the Switzerland border. The Western Front was in a worse state than Gallipoli and many of the survivors from Gallipoli died there during the next two years.

1915 is the year we will always remember as the year so many soldiers lost their lives, bravely fighting for what they believed in. As stated by the main character, Archy, in the 1981 film *Gallipoli*, "You just had to be a part of it". Lest we forget.

Lucy's essay demonstrates the capacity of a Year 10 student to have a secure grasp of historical empathy. In Table 1.2 I have identified where Lucy's writing illustrates this point and (occasionally) where it could be developed further.

Table 1.2. The affective and cognitive dimensions of historical empathy displayed in Lucy's essay

Cognitive dimension	Examples from Lucy's essay	My comments
Building historical contextual knowledge	"Most of the men settled in New Zealand during the time of the First World War had grown up on the isolated islands, and so the thought of adventure appealed to them."	Lucy's grasp of context could be developed further so that she provides a broader picture of why soldiers held thoughts of adventure.
Being aware of the past as being different from the present	"1915 is the year we will always remember as the year so many soldiers lost their lives, bravely fighting for what they believed in."	Lucy is able to stand back and allude to "we" in the present remembering those in the past who were fighting for a different set of beliefs.
Tying interpretations of the past to evidence.	"Joining the war was 'the thing to do at the time'. Soldiers joined up because it was popular." (Vic Nicolson)	Lucy makes a great deal of use of the veterans' reflections. She takes these at face value but does conclude that there were many reasons why men joined up.
Affective dimension		
Using imagination to recognise appropriate feelings	"The soldiers wanted to fight for their country and its rights, believing they would return to New Zealand as heroes."	Lucy does not use imagination as a 'flight of fancy' or a 'let's pretend' version of history, but instead ties it closely to the evidence she has selected.
Listening to and entertaining other points of view	"The final, but not the only other reason, as it varies with different people, is because they were patriotic and loved their country."	The open-mindedness in Lucy's writing reflects a willingness to accept that the men's motivations were diverse, and (possibly) a concern not to pre-judge concepts such as patriotism.
Being caring, sensitive and tolerant towards other people	"1915 is the year we will always remember as the year so many soldiers lost their lives, bravely fighting for what they believed in. As stated by the main character, Archy, in the 1981 film *Gallipoli*, 'You just had to be a part of it'. Lest we forget."	Here Lucy sensitively refers to the importance of remembering what happened at Gallipoli. However, she does not discuss why using the words of a fictional character such as Archy is problematic.

'How might we help students get better at historical empathy?' is a question that is relevant to all history teachers. Here I look at three possible approaches to addressing this question. One way would be to approach progression as a sequence of levels, rather like Ashby and Lee's (1987) typology, which uses five levels of historical empathy, ranging from the naïve to the sophisticated.

Table 1.3. Ashby and Lee's stages of historical empathy

Level	Description
1	Students believe the past to be unknowable and that people who inhabited the past were less bright than people today.
2	Students use stereotypes to explain the past.
3	Using everyday empathy, students can imagine what it was like for people in the past but through the lens of the present.
4	Students understand, in specific situations, that the past was different and that people's values were different.
5	Students understand, in the broader contexts of whole societies, that the past was different and that people's values were different.

Source: Ashby & Lee, 1987

This typology is a useful planning tool, potentially helping teachers to write objectives. It also signals to teachers what to look out for as students grapple with learning historical empathy. As Lee and Shemilt put it, typologies help teachers to identify "the break points" in students' thinking (2004, p. 29). However, as Ashby and Lee make clear, typologies are not intended to chart individual progression, largely because students will frequently be at more than one level at any given time. Equally, Culpin (1994) makes a good point by highlighting that in such typologies one level does not always relate particularly well to the adjacent level.

A second approach to progression, which is also linear but used to gauge the progress of individuals, is the achievement criteria used in New Zealand's public examination system, the National Certificate of Educational Achievement (NCEA). These levels show progression as a relatively straightforward shift from less to more in-depth understanding, as illustrated in Table 1.4.

Table 1.4. NCEA achievement criteria: An example from achievement standard 91004

Achievement	Merit	Excellence
Demonstrate *understanding* of different perspectives of people in an historical event of significance to New Zealanders.	Demonstrate *in-depth understanding* of different perspectives of people in an historical event of significance to New Zealanders.	Demonstrate *comprehensive understanding* of different perspectives of people in an historical event of significance to New Zealanders.

This is useful if the aim is for students to recognise different perspectives and if progress in history is considered to be a matter of fostering greater depth. This could, however, be a too-narrow description of progress if the intention is for students to learn about historical empathy across both its cognitive and affective dimensions.

A third approach has been suggested by Vermeulen (2000), who sees progress as a non-linear process, whereby students become expert at mastering a wide range of concepts and the inter-connections between them. Vermeulen likens this to the "growth of a spider's web" (2000, p. 36). This approach would mean trying to bring together the cognitive and affective criteria related to historical empathy. For instance, with care, sensitivity and tolerance comes greater understanding of historical context and the ability to make better sense of the evidence. As Vermeulen also points out, the advantage of this approach is that it does not define progression as being solely about students' learning more and more detail. Rather, like Marshall's (2004) work in the teaching of English, it promotes progression in terms of students moving towards broad horizons. It also avoids what the Australian educationalist Royce Sadler (2007) calls "decomposition":

> if you break something into pieces, whatever originally held it together has to be either supplied or satisfactorily substituted if the sense of the whole is to be restored. (2007, p. 390)

For those teaching history in New Zealand schools, this may mean trying not to lose sight of history as a whole, or what Sadler (2009) calls a subject's "guild knowledge". Progression is made when students acquire this guild knowledge and become part of a history community (the guild), which can judge what constitutes sophisticated historical empathy. This could be achieved by looking at lots of examples of how students write about historical empathy (as in Lucy's essay). In this way, it is the use of student exemplars, possibly taken at different stages of the teaching sequence, that would provide the best gauge of progression.

Conclusion

The aim of this chapter has been to describe how historical empathy might be taught in the history classroom. In doing so, it has made the case for interpreting historical empathy as a concept with both cognitive and affective dimensions. While acknowledging that historical empathy can be a confusing and contested concept, this chapter has put forward a practical model of how it can be taught within the context of New Zealand history. It has also described how teachers might approach the assessment of historical empathy and gauge student progression.

References

Ashby, R., & Lee, P. J. (1987). Children's concepts of empathy and understanding in history. In C. Portal (Ed.), *The history curriculum for teachers* (pp. 62–88). London, UK: The Falmer Press.

Barton, K. C., &Levstik, L. S. (2004). *Teaching history for the common good*. Mahwah, NJ: Lawrence Erlbaum Associates.

Boyak, N., & Tolerton, J. (1990). *In the shadow of war: New Zealand soldiers talk about World War One and their lives*. Auckland: Penguin.

Brooks, S. (2009). Historical empathy in the social studies classroom: A review of the literature. *Journal of Social Studies Research, 33*(2), 213–234.

Burke, V., & Waru, R. (Producers). (2005). Episode 8: The price of empire. *Frontier of dreams*. Auckland: TVNZ.

Cessford, C. (2010, 25 April). *Anzac at war: Peter Pederson*, with Chris Laidlaw. New Zealand: Radio New Zealand National [podcast]. Retrieved 15 July 2010 from http://www.radionz.co.nz/national/programmes/sunday/audio/2276577/anzacs-at-war-peter-pedersen

Chamberlain, J. (Ed.). (2008). *Shrapnel and semaphore: A signaller's diary from Gallipoli*. Auckland: New Holland Publishers.

Cormack, C. (2009). *Macmillan wall charts: Anzac day*. South Yarra, VIC: Macmillan.

Cowan, J. (1926) (2011). *Māori in the great war*. Christchurch: Willsonscott.

Culpin, C. (1994). Making progress in history. In H. Bourdillon (Ed.), *Teaching History* (pp. 126-152). London, UK: Routledge.

Denton, A. (Presenter). (2007). *Gallipoli: Brothers in arms* [documentary]. Sydney, New South Wales: ABC Television.

Department of Education and Science. (1985). *History in the primary and secondary years: An HMI view.* London, UK: Her Majesty's Stationery Office.

Donovan, D. (2005). *Anzac memories: Images from the Great War.* Auckland: New Holland Publishers.

Donovan, M.S. & Bransford, J.D. (2005). *How students learn: History in the classroom.* Washington, DC: The National Academies Press.

Downey, M.T. (1996). *Writing to learn history in the intermediate grades.* Berkeley, CA: National Center for the Study of Writing and Literacy.

Dulberg, N. (2002). *Engaging in history: Empathy and perspective taking in children's historical thinking.* Paper presented at the annual meeting of the American Educational Research Association.

Endacott, J.L. (2010). Reconsidering affective engagement in historical empathy. *Theory and Research in Social Education, 38*(1), 6-49.

Foster, S. J. (2001). Historical empathy in theory and practice: Some final thoughts. In O. L. Davis, E. A. Yeager, & S. J. Foster (Eds.), *Historical empathy and perspective taking in the social studies* (pp. 167-182). Lanham, MD: Rowman and Littlefield.

Gaddis, J.L. (2002). *The landscape of history: How historians map the past.* New York, NY: Oxford University Press.

Hexter, J.H. (1971). *The history primer.* New York, NY: Basic Books.

Hoffman, M.L. (2000). *Empathy and moral development: Implications for caring and justice.* New York, NY: Cambridge University Press.

King, M. (2003). *The Penguin history of New Zealand.* Auckland: Penguin.

Lee, P.J. (1984). Historical imagination. In A.K. Dickinson, P.J. Lee, & P.J. Rogers (Eds.), *Learning history* (pp. 85-116). London, UK: Heinemann.

Lee, P.J., & Shemilt, D. (2004). "I just wish we could go back in the past and find out what really happened": Progression in understanding about historical accounts. *Teaching History, 117,* 25-31.

Marcus, A. S. (2007). Students making sense of the past: "It's almost like living the event". In A.S. Marcus (Ed.), *Celluloid blackboard: Teaching history with film* (pp. 121-167). Charlotte, NC: Information Age Publishing.

Marshall, B. (2004). Goals or horizons—the conundrum of progression in English: Or a possible way of understanding formative assessment in English. *The Curriculum Journal, 15*(2), 101-113.

McWilliams, N. (2004). *Psychoanalytic psychotherapy: A practitioner's guide*. New York, NY: The Guilford Press.

Meier, D. (1996). Suppose that ... *Phi Delta Kappan*, December, 271-276.

Ministry of Education.(2007). *The New Zealand curriculum*. Wellington: Learning Media.

Pugsley, C. (1984). *Gallipoli: The New Zealand story*. Auckland: Hodder and Stoughton.

Rees, P. (2008). *The other Anzacs: Nurses at war, 1914-1918*. Crows Nest, NSW: Allen & Unwin.

Sadler, D.R. (2007). Perils in the meticulous specification of goals and assessment criteria. *Assessment in Education*, 3(14), 387-392.

Sadler, D.R. (2009). Grade integrity and the representation of academic achievement. *Studies in Higher Education*, 34(7), 807-826.

Seixas, P., & Peck, C. (2004). Teaching historical thinking. In A. Sears & I. Wright (Eds.), *Challenges and prospects for Canadian social studies* (pp. 109-117). Vancouver, BC: Pacific Educational Press.

Shadbolt, M. (1988). *Voices of Gallipoli*. Auckland: Hodder and Stoughton.

Shemilt, D. (1984). Beauty and the philosopher: Empathy in history and classroom. In A.K. Dickinson, P.J. Lee, & P.J. Rogers (Eds.), *Learning history* (pp. 39-84). London, UK: Heinemann.

Slote, M. (2007). *The ethics of care and empathy*. New York, NY: Routledge.

Slote, M. (2010). *Moral sentimentalism*. Oxford, UK: Oxford University Press.

Taylor, T. (2011, 6 May). *From bad history to real history: Issues in developing historical literacy*. Lecture presented at the Faculty of Education, University of Auckland, Auckland, New Zealand.

Van Drie, J., & Van Boxtel, C. (2008). Historical reasoning: Towards a framework for analyzing students' reasoning about the past. *Educational Psychology Review*, 20, 87-110.

Vermeulen, E. (2000). What is progress in history? *Teaching History*, 98, 35-41.

Weir, P. (Director). (1981) *Gallipoli* [feature film]. Hollywood, CA: Paramount.

Wineburg, S. (2001). *Historical thinking and other unnatural acts: Charting the future of teaching the past*. Philadelphia, PA: Temple University Press.

Wineburg, S. (2007). *Unnatural and essential: The nature of historical thinking*. Teaching History, 129, 6-12.

"I realised then that history is a power in the present. Ignore the narratives and agency of people in the past, and you are likely to ignore their descendants."

Anne Salmond[1]

---

1 A. Salmond. (2006). Ancestral places. In K. Gentry & G. Mclean (Eds.), *Heartlands: New Zealand historians write about where history happened* (pp. 135–144). Albany: Penguin Group.

CHAPTER 2

Pictorial pedagogies:
Interpreting historical images as evidence

Barbara Ormond

Barbara Ormond is a senior lecturer in the Faculty of Education, The University of Auckland. She lectures in the disciplines of history, art history and social sciences for secondary education. She taught at Selwyn College in Auckland for 18 years and, at a national level, has held leadership roles in art history, including national moderator and scholarship examiner. She brings a cross-disciplinary perspective to her research into visual historical evidence and is the author of *The Iconography of Visual Culture and Pedagogical Approaches to Seeing: Illustrated Prints Pertaining to Religious Issues in Early Modern England*.

Barbara can be contacted at: b.ormond@auckland.ac.nz

Introduction

The study of historical images has grown in importance under the umbrella of an evidence-based inquiry approach. There is a developing realisation that exploring the visual culture of peoples of the past provides a unique perspective on societies as they were seen through the eyes of artists, illustrators and publishers. Pictorial evidence can support, contradict or nuance understanding gained through other forms of evidence, and can reveal ideas that may not be stated explicitly in text.

The expectation that students of history will engage in interpreting visual evidence, such as paintings, photographs and digital images, is part of the increasing emphasis placed on students acting like historians in delving into source material and contextualising it by referring to multiple sources. However, while visual forms of evidence appear regularly in examination papers and are used as historical sources for inquiry, pedagogies that target the skills of visual interpretation are not always given sufficient emphasis by teachers. There may be an assumption that students live in a visual age and therefore have an innate ability to read images accurately. However, imagery that derives from unfamiliar times and places creates challenges. Through the use of targeted learning strategies, students can be encouraged to develop insightful readings of visual evidence, leading to improved historical understanding and confidence in interpreting a range of media.

The pictorial turn

Michael Coventry and his co-authors have coined the phrases "pictorial turn", to describe the shift in history teaching towards investigating visual culture, and "pedagogical turn", to highlight the shift towards enabling students to think historically (Coventry et al., 2006, p. 1372). The pictorial turn recognises the way in which history teaching has largely moved beyond the practice of using pictures to show what things looked like, or to confirm historical knowledge already gleaned from written sources, in order to focus on investigating visual evidence as a contribution to enhancing historical understanding. Frank and Jean Colson, Ross Parry and Andrew Sawyer argue that

> Now that history has promoted its images from secondary illustration to primary evidence ... it is perhaps time to explore how in this new leading role it can allow us to see very different stories of the past. (Bolvig & Lindley, 2003, p. 207)

A number of New Zealand historians have led the way in positioning historical imagery at the forefront of their histories. Judith Binney, Gillian Chaplin and Craig Wallace used photographic evidence as a fundamental part of their investigations for the publication *Mihaia:*

The Prophet Rua Kenana and His Community at Maungapohatu in 1979. The study comprised over 350 photographs, and Binney commented on the originality of the approach at the time, saying that "No work of this kind has been undertaken before in New Zealand, nor indeed, has much been done elsewhere" (Binney, Chaplin, & Wallace, 1979, p. 10). The importance of photographs as historical evidence was also notable in *Looking Back: A Photographic History of New Zealand*, by Keith Sinclair and Wendy Harrex, who commented in 1978 that while "In modern times historians have concerned themselves mainly with documentary records", the photographic record is "as vivid and revealing" (Sinclair & Harrex, 1978, p. 5).

The importance of visual language is recognised as a key competency in *The New Zealand Curriculum*, which seeks to develop students' awareness that "people ... produce texts of all kinds: written, oral/aural, and visual" (Ministry of Education, 2007, p. 12). There is also specific reference to "Using ... symbols ... and making meaning of the codes in which knowledge is expressed" (p. 12), and sign, symbol and iconographical conventions are important contributors to meaning in visual forms of expression. This validates the need for more robust pedagogies to help students acquire the tools to interpret images in relation to the representational modes of a particular time and place, and shows that text and image should both be given recognition.

NCEA similarly acknowledges the importance of visual imagery through assessment practices. In history, which is commonly available at the senior levels of New Zealand secondary schools, the assessment programme, through the Achievement Standards, specifically includes a source interpretation standard at each year level. Within the explanatory notes in these Achievement Standards is a list of examples of sources, which includes "pictures, [and] ... cartoons" alongside other forms of historical evidence such as "documents, [and] ... maps" (NZQA, 2010, AS91231, p. 2). Examination questions can require discussion of concepts such as reliability or bias, intent and motivation, and continuity and change in relation to the sources.

Under examination conditions, students are expected to be able to interpret sources they are unlikely to have encountered before in relation to contexts that may be unfamiliar. An examiner may select any historical context to assess source interpretation skills, and normally the context will differ from topics the students have learned during the year. Because insightful analysis of visual imagery often requires knowledge of the historical period, visual culture, and circumstances in which an image was produced, this practice of interpreting sources under limited knowledge conditions does present some challenges. To explain actions and viewpoints expressed through imagery, it is often necessary to understand an artist's intent and to recognise figures, objects or symbols. The focus on visual analytical skills does, however, give weight to the value of developing students' visual acuity through methodologies that can be applied to a wide variety of pictorial evidence.

Skills in interpreting sources are also inherent in the internally assessed research standards for each year level. Students carry out an investigation and follow historical processes that include "identifying possible sources and how they may be useful" (NZQA, 2010, AS91001, p. 1), and "selecting evidence from a variety of sources, including both primary and secondary sources" (p. 2). Such approaches offer students the opportunity to experience history through adopting features of a historian's practice. However, educator Keith Barton urges caution in using primary sources. While recognising that "Using primary sources engages students in authentic historical inquiry" (Barton, 2005, p. 748), he argues that in practice the opportunity to engage sufficiently with sources to satisfactorily investigate a topic is normally beyond the capabilities of students in the timeframes allowed.

In the case of visual images, the same cautionary approach is needed. Understanding of the past is more often developed not by reference to the occasional image but by working within knowledge gained through a range of images and through recognising the importance of historical and production contexts for visual imagery. Barton also identifies as problematic the potential for students to believe that "Primary sources are more reliable than secondary sources" (Barton, 2005, p. 746). It is only through consideration of the purposes and nature of the visual culture of a particular time and place that students can begin to evaluate the sources and reliably interpret the motivations behind, and meanings of, the visual imagery. Nevertheless, using visual evidence is not only a requirement for assessment purposes, but is also fundamental to a holistic approach to exploring the breadth of historical evidence. Incorporating imagery into learning may also serve pedagogical ends in terms of making ideas, historical events and personalities more comprehensible and memorable.

Another fundamental concept that students should understand is that although images have dominant meanings that are likely to have been shared by viewers of the time and place in which they were produced, they may also have deliberate or unintended multiple meanings and will be interpreted differently by different viewers. Deriving meaning involves a complex relationship, whereby the maker creates an image having certain intended messages in mind, and then the viewer experiences that image and brings their own knowledge and attitudes to it. Marita Sturken and Lisa Cartwright argue that "meaning does not reside within images, but is produced at the moment that they are consumed by and circulate among viewers" (Sturken & Cartwright, 2001, p. 7). They also note that images "rarely 'speak' to everyone universally" (p. 7), and this is particularly relevant to studying images that are far removed in time and place from our own experience. If students set out believing that they must give a single, accurate interpretation of an image, then they may regard the task of interpretation as beyond them. However, if students recognise that their interpretations can differ and may be valid, they are more likely to confidently proceed in making meaning from what they see.

Challenges for students

Historical evidence of any kind presents challenges to students, as each piece of evidence represents just a piece of a jigsaw of historical understanding. The issues of determining an item's evidential weight, reliability and positioning in relation to a point of view require substantial student judgement. While the interpretation of pictorial evidence also requires these considerations, there are factors that are specific to, or prominent in relation to, the analysis of imagery. To understand the rhetoric of an image, students need to be aware of the stylistic and narrative conventions that prevailed in the era in which the artist produced the image.

For example, knowledge of the stylistic characteristics and purposes and practices of artists in mid-19th century New Zealand gives clues to the reliability of images from this period in terms of providing an accurate representation of European settlement. Once students realise that many of the artists who illustrated the early colonial period were amateur painters whose role was to produce illustrations to promote colonial settlement, then the lens through which one interprets such images changes. The viewer begins to look for elements of propaganda—a shift away from what these places may have been like or looked like to what the artist wished to convey.

These 'topographical' landscape paintings provided information potential settlers wished to know about: the lie of the land, the availability of fresh water, safe harbours, friendly natives, and signs of progress in the built environment. These artists conveyed, in relatively simplistic terms, an image of land cleared and settled with fences, roads, and comforting houses and churches. They also adopted stylistic practices that would enhance the landscape, such as using panoramic views to convey a sense of the vast availability of suitable land, and clear warm light to convey a temperate climate. Hamish Keith notes that this propaganda element went further in that the lithographs made from these watercolour paintings, which were used in publications by the New Zealand Company, were further cleaned up and given captions such as "emphasising peaceful encounters" (Keith, 2007, p. 56). The process of creating lithographs from the original watercolours involved redrawing the paintings onto stone slabs, and these were then used to create the printed reproductions. The lithographer could, therefore, make alterations to the original to create images purpose-fit for encouraging settlers.

In William Fox's *New Plymouth in 1849*, the panoramic view facilitates the inclusion of a large number of elements that might be attractive to a prospective settler. The solid structures of houses and an Anglican church are scattered through the landscape. There is easy access to the sea and a calm bay suitable for mooring. A substantial road also gives access by land, and the two figures—one on horseback, the other walking alongside—are familiar signposts of human contentment. Suitability for farming is emphasised through the inclusion of cattle and fenced pastures. The scenic beauty of the landscape is evident in snow-capped Taranaki/

Mount Egmont, while wilderness areas such as the bush at the base of the mountain are distant and simplified into non-threatening features that can be overlooked. A student encountering such imagery for the first time may glean meaning from the indicators of progress, but may give little consideration to the deliberate schematising of the landscape, which ensures there is no focus on inaccessible land areas or the potential for the weather to pound these open coastal settlements.

Figure 2.1. William Fox, *New Plymouth In 1849*
Watercolour, 165 x 1015 mm, Hocken Pictorial Collections, Dunedin. [Acc 13,378]

To enable students to understand the conventions of the watercolour images of this period, and the role propaganda played in selecting and ordering the imagery, students could be given several images from the same period to investigate and compare. For example, if students were to analyse the evidence of early settlement using examples from William Fox (Figure 2.1), Charles Heaphy (Figure 2.2) and Emma Wicksteed (Figure 2.3), images that range in date from 1841 to 1849, they may come to realise that illustrations of orderliness, moderate climatic conditions and prosperity, and indicators of the potential for future growth of settlements, fall within the conventions for illustrating New Zealand, particularly where those images were used in the service of the New Zealand Company. Iain Sharp comments that Heaphy's view of Wellington

> is one of the most assured pieces of advertising … It emphasises the progress that has already been made: good roads in place, sturdy buildings constructed, a fine harbour affording excellent communication by sea. Supported by first-rate agricultural opportunities (those cows and goats in the foreground), the immigrant can enjoy a pleasant life, riding, boating and strolling. (Sharp, 2008, p. 63)

Figure 2.2. Charles Heaphy, *View of a part of the town of Wellington, New Zealand, looking towards the south east, comprising about one-third of water-frontage, September 1841*
Watercolour, 442 x 620 mm, Alexander Turnbull Library, Wellington, New Zealand [Ref C-025-009].

Similarly, *The Town of New Plymouth*, by Emma Wicksteed, the wife of a New Zealand Company agent living in New Plymouth between 1842 and 1847, is a civilised panoramic view painted from the garden of her home. She depicted the key topographical features of Taranaki/Mount Egmont and hills, along with plentiful land, substantial homes, the Kings Arms Inn, and cows and a bullock cart on the road. A lithograph was made from Wicksteed's sketch and published in 1845 in Edward Jerningham Wakefield's highly successful book *Adventure in New Zealand*. Like his father, Edward Gibbon Wakefield, Edward Jerningham Wakefield was an employee of the New Zealand Company, whom Ronda Cooper described as a "propagandist and apologist" for the company (Cooper, 2010).

Figure 2.3. Emma Wicksteed, *The Town of New Plymouth, 1843*
Lithograph (detail 237 x 492), Alexander Turnbull Library, Wellington, New Zealand [PUBL-0011-09-2].

While paintings by Fox, Heaphy and other artists of the 1840s often supported the goals of the New Zealand Company through their carefully engineered images, not all artists had the same purpose. George French Angas, for example, was a travelling artist who, while self-taught, was a professional artist whose goal was to depict "the natives and scenery of New Zealand … with unexaggerated truth and fidelity" (Bell, 1992, p. 11). His paintings are generally regarded as fairly accurate and less driven by colonial desires to promote the benefits of New Zealand as a destination. Students can easily misinterpret the purposes of images if the circumstances under which artists created their images are not known.

Keith Barton asserts that "Historians use a 'sourcing heuristic' to evaluate bias and reliability" (Barton, 2005, p. 747). He refers to the way in which sources are used in history education in order to debate their trustworthiness, and argues that this is not the way historians approach sources: historians often deliberately look for sources that show bias rather than evaluating them in terms of their bias. The relevance of this viewpoint to the interpretation of early images of New Zealand is that students need to keep in mind that not all the artists conveying early colonial New Zealand would have had a deliberate intent or bias. They

Figure 2.4. George French Angas, *Motupoi Pah and Roto-aire Lake: Tongariro in the distance*, 1847
Lithograph, 232 x 324 mm, Alexander Turnbull Library, Wellington, New Zealand. [B-080-028]

may well have represented the landscape in accordance with prevailing conventions or for picturesque reasons without deliberately placing an individual bias upon their work. For example, despite Emma Wicksteed's links to the New Zealand Company, her original sketch may have been, in her opinion, an accurate record of an attractive landscape viewed from her home. It is plausible that the interpretation of the bias or propaganda may instead derive, firstly, from its appearance in a publication linked to the New Zealand Company, and secondly, from any alterations to the image that Wakefield may have required at the point the lithograph was made.

Interpreting visual evidence

Art historians use methods for reading images that take account of the subject of the image, iconographical schema, the way the image is composed, patronage and the intended audience, and the stylistic features prevalent at the time it was produced. While these aspects are not always relevant for studying a particular visual culture of the past, history teachers can learn from the art historian's methods, adapting them to develop systematic processes to facilitate interpretation of imagery from a given time or place. Practising visual analysis skills may be particularly beneficial for enabling students to read images that are unfamiliar, as they are likely to be in the NCEA examinations for the source interpretation Achievement Standards. Although many history teachers employ a recognised process for interpreting cartoons, whereby students identify people, objects, symbols and actions before moving on to consider a collective interpretation of those features, such approaches do not appear to have been widely developed or consistently applied in relation to pictorial evidence. To take students on a journey of discovery through an image, features such as the setting, mood, gestures, medium and purposes in producing the art works become important considerations (see Table 2.1).

Such an approach cannot guarantee to deliver an appropriate reading, but organising a sequence of steps in a way that ensures a careful treasure hunt of the features has the potential to enable students to make connections between what they see and the meanings conveyed through the image. By repeatedly using the same step-by-step analysis to interpret a range of images, students acquire the mental processes needed to deal with various images. A methodology such as this goes some way towards addressing Michael Coventry's concern that "we have few conventions for reading images as historical sources" (Coventry et al., 2006, p. 4).

The role of media in pictorial evidence

A further challenge for students interpreting pictorial evidence is the role medium plays in the reading of images. Students can be encouraged to develop an awareness of the differences in characteristics of various media through comparing, for example, a photograph and a painting of the same scene, and considering how different interpretations arise despite similarities in imagery. Using two images of the settlement of Parihaka—a photograph and a watercolour painting, both from 1881 (Figures 2.5 and 2.6)—it becomes clear that both painter and photographer were positioned in an almost identical elevated position to look down

Table 2.1. Interpreting pictorial evidence: A journey through an image

	Journey questions	Fill in your clues
Identify objects and setting.	Which are the most prominent objects in the visual image? What other objects can you see? What is the setting or location?	
Identify figures.	Can you recognise any of the figures?	
Identify written clues.	Does the image have a caption, any accompanying text, or date?	
Describe the mood.	What mood is being conveyed? (e.g. positive, threatening, heroic, appearance of being commonplace)	
Describe the subject.	What actions are taking place? What do gestures tell you about the participant's thoughts? Explain the interrelationship between objects, the figures and their setting.	
What medium is used?	Can you recognise the medium? (e.g. is it an oil painting which is normally a one-off image, or a print which may have been produced for mass publication?)	
Bring context into play.	What knowledge do you have about the time period, place, or historical circumstances? (use that knowledge to explain the actions, objects and figures) Who is the artist? Why did he/she create the image?	
Recognising underlying ideas and drawing conclusions.	What key message(s), and/or underlying ideas, do you think the artist wishes to convey? How does the artist convey these ideas? How reliable is the imagery as a reflection of historical circumstances or viewpoints?	

upon the roofs of the whare, and that both artists chose to illustrate the same portion of landscape, yet the overall impression of the Parihaka settlement differs. The watercolour medium enabled clear delineation of buildings and objects, such as the wagon in the foreground, while the pale hues prevalent in watercolour project an overall sense of calm. The impression is of a settlement that is well organised, clean, with neat rows of whare and well-formed paths and roads. The clear view of Taranaki/Mount Egmont provides a glorious backdrop, which enhances the sense of wellbeing for the settlement of Parihaka. In contrast, a black-and-white photograph, with the limitations of long exposure times and the grainy quality of early prints, obscures some of the detail and presents a picture of a more crowded, less planned settlement. Taranaki/Mount Egmont is not clearly visible in the photograph, so the viewer focuses entirely upon the settlement. Features such as the paths, roads and garden that are readable as tidy in the watercolour could be mistaken for muddy areas in the photograph, and the inference students may draw, without knowledge of the medium, is of a doomed Māori community, downtrodden and waiting for the inevitable invasion of troops and confiscation of lands.

Figure 2.5. *View of Parihaka Pa, at the time of the assault by the armed constabulary,* November 1881
Photograph by William Andrews Collis, Alexander Turnbull Library, Wellington, New Zealand. [G-1072-10x8]

Figure 2.6. George Clarendon Beale, *Parihaka*, 1881
Watercolour, Puke Ariki. [A65.651]

To illustrate differences determined by media, students could be put into groups and each group given only one of the two Parihaka images. The students could then use a visual analysis process (such as that provided in Table 2.1) to glean all they can from the image and draw conclusions, or they could be given specific guidance or questions for particular images (see Table 2.2). After finishing this activity, the two groups come together and explain their interpretations of the different images. There is likely to be surprise when the students realise their interpretations differ—perhaps significantly. Through this co-operative learning task students can gain understandings which enable them to engage in the critical thinking required for the Excellence-level criterion for Achievement Standard 2.3 (AS91231), *Examine sources of an historical event that is of significance to New Zealanders* (*NZQA*, 2011, p. 1). In this standard, the criterion for Excellence involves comprehensively examining sources, which is explained as follows:

> *Comprehensively examine sources* involves using one or more historical skill(s) to show perceptive understanding of sources. Showing perceptive understanding involves '*reading between the lines*' to draw conclusions that go beyond the immediately obvious, and/or to raise relevant questions ... that demonstrate a high degree of engagement with the source. It could involve selecting and explaining evidence with an awareness of the limitations of either the evidence or the basis for making assumptions about it. (p. 2)

With an understanding of the differing characteristics of particular visual media, students can gain a greater appreciation of the limitations of the media under study and of underlying issues such as reliability of evidence and the way artists' manipulation, creativity and selectivity can alter perceptions of historical evidence.

Table 2.2. Student activity: Comparing images of the Parihaka settlement

Images of Parihaka — Instructions for Group Activity

Discuss the image you have been given and answer the following questions. Select one person in your group to record the answers.

What can you see in this image? (e.g. objects, buildings, geographical features)

What can you interpret about the settlement of Parihaka from this image?

How reliable, or useful, might this image be for an historian studying Parihaka? Explain your views.

When you have completed your analysis of the image and recorded your ideas, join with another group who has been studying the other image of Parihaka and compare your interpretations.

Ideally, to draw appropriate conclusions students need to engage in the complex task of integrating multiple sources of information and, in particular, moving between interpretive written accounts and the images. David Jaffee has observed that

> Studying the way my students looked at visual materials, I realised that word and image needed to be reunited ... Students needed more scaffolding so that they could learn to move between historical, literary and visual materials. (Coventry et al., 2006, pp. 1378-80)

Jaffee concluded that "When students encounter images, they often offer incomplete readings, demonstrating difficulty integrating their insightful visual readings with contextual historical understanding" (p. 1378). Pedagogical approaches need to address the likely shortfall between students' interpretations of an image and the social, political, historical and production contexts in which it was made. To achieve this, students could be given a mini-archive of resources, both visual and written, to explore in some depth a selected historical issue, idea, event or concept. The mini-archive could comprise primary and secondary sources relating to contextual factors, and historians' and contemporaries' perspectives. Students would consider the range of sources to explore the visual images in context and determine matters such as the relevance and evidential weight of the sources to draw conclusions about meaning and intent.

When attempting to interpret visual cultures from distant times or places, the particular modes of representation employed by artists may be unfamiliar and create barriers to understanding. Representational conventions develop in relation to cultural and historical contexts, and the signs and symbols that form part of the representational code are normally a commonly understood verbal signature for those living in a given place or era. For students encountering such imagery for the first time, such symbols and representational approaches need to be explained. If, for example, students were to investigate early modern English prints they would need to know about the frequently used symbols and signs that encode key messages. Students should also be aware of the differences in production and audience for woodcuts in comparison with engravings, and an understanding that images were repeatedly used and put to different political, moral or religious purposes rather than produced as one-off, specific visuals to illustrate a particular narrative or event. It would also be beneficial for them to have some insight into the censorship that operated to limit craftsmen's approaches to subject matter. Without some knowledge of the particular characteristics of visual cultures it is difficult to see the way imagery has been constructed to make meaning.

To bring together source analysis skills and knowledge as diverse as representational conventions, production contexts, historical contexts and perspectives, a three-level guide can be used. This learning strategy was originally designed to enable students to access and comprehend texts, but it is also valuable when adapted for interpreting visual images. It encourages a close reading of images and debate on finer points of interpretation.

A three-level guide takes the form of a series of statements written by the teacher. The statements are written in a manner that comprehends a piece of text, or, suitably adapted, interprets visual images. The statements are divided into three levels:

- level one—a straightforward reading of what can be seen in the visual
- level two—an interpretation of the meaning of the visual imagery
- level three—an evaluation of the ideas underlying the visual.

Level three can also be used to look at what an artist intended in their work. Students tick the correct statements after reading the image and they have to justify their decisions. This method ensures that students carefully scrutinise the visual, identifying both what can be seen and the underlying ideas expressed within it.

The three-level reading of the image is reinforced by a three-step approach to reporting responses to each statement.

- Step 1: The individual student reads the visual and ticks the statements they believe to be accurate. Only ticks are used (not crosses) because some statements may be written to be partially correct and partially incorrect.
- Step 2: The students pair up and compare their answers. Where they differ they have to justify their decision, or agree to alter it if convinced by their partner's arguments.
- Step 3: The students form into groups of four (or this can be done as a whole class) and compare their answers. Where they differ they have to justify their decisions, or agree to alter their decisions if convinced by the group's arguments.

The teacher uses their own researched knowledge of the image, and their estimation of how much is likely to be noticed and understood about the visual initially by the students, to determine the information that is included in the statements. Teaching context and content alongside interpretation can be largely controlled by the teacher since, in writing the statements, the teacher can provide contextual information or historical and visual detail that he/she believes is important for the students to know and understand. Through statements that identify particular features of the image, the teacher can also lead students in a treasure hunt to find objects, actions or relationships that are significant to the interpretation of the particular image.

Table 2.3 is an example of a three-level guide written for a painting by Gustavus von Tempsky, *British camp surprised by Maoris who were driven off with heavy losses* (Figure 2.7). The methodology of a three-level guide works best when a straightforward statement is used as the first statement at level one, such as "Captain Witchell, on his grey steed, is about to swing his sword at the Māori warrior". A number of statements should also be written in a manner that encourages debate on whether or not they are entirely accurate. For example, the statement in level one that "British soldiers are outnumbered by Māori rebels" can be argued. Von Tempsky shows two soldiers and three Māori involved in the immediate conflict with one further Māori rebel nearby. However, the artist implies that more British cavalry are close to hand as two are seen ascending the hill. Such a statement may alert students to the problems of literal readings of imagery and demonstrate how artists are selective in the figures and objects they include and focus on.

Although students may not have any specific knowledge of this event in the New Zealand Wars, a number of statements are designed to encourage scrutiny of significant viewpoints and historical interpretations. The first statement in level two, "The Māori rebels are depicted as noble, brave fighters", can be read either in the affirmative or in the negative, but taps into debates at the time and since about how Māori were viewed by Europeans. Commentaries about their fighting prowess and courage abound alongside the many written references to Māori as "savages". The three-level guide can also be designed to provide information that students would not be expected to know or be able to interpret. For example, "Von Tempsky follows 19th-century conventions in depicting cavalry with the horse rearing and a heroic fighter taking up a dominant position" is a statement that may not be easily answered by students, but it is framed in a manner that suggests it is likely to be accurate. The ideas related to the statement can then be discussed as a class, and students who have studied art history may be able to inform their peers about relevant comparative examples, such as Gericault's *The Charging Cuirassier* (c. 1812).

Figure 2.7. Gustavus von Tempsky, *British camp surprised by Maoris who were driven off with heavy losses*, c.1866
Watercolour, 228 x 288 mm, Auckland War Memorial Museum. [PD 29(1)]

The strategy of the three-level guide leads students through the interpretation of an image and enables those of mixed abilities to access the imagery. Because students do not have to develop the statements themselves, they are not hindered by varying competency with language and can concentrate on looking and interpreting.

Conclusion

Although images are increasingly being promoted to a position of greater respect in historical research and teaching, the development of methodologies for interpreting visual culture and utilising imagery in educational fields is still relatively young. This chapter has identified

Table 2.3. Three-level guide: Gustavus von Tempsky, *British camp surprised by Maoris who were driven off with heavy losses*, c. 1866.

THREE-LEVEL GUIDE

British camp surprised by Maoris who were driven off with heavy losses **by Gustavus von Tempsky, Watercolour, 228 x 288 mm, collection of The Auckland War Memorial Museum c.1866**

Student Instructions: Look carefully at the painting and tick the statements that you agree with. Work individually, and once you have finished discuss your answers with another student. Amend any answer if you are convinced by the other student's argument.

Background: On 24 January 1865 British soldiers set up camp near the small Māori village of Nukumaru. They then moved to occupy an area of bush close to the village and were fired upon by Māori who took up a position at the edge of the bush. The following day the Māori attacked outlying picket positions near the camp and, while they were driven back into the bush, there was one further encounter between the Māori and the British Royal Artillery and cavalry.

Major Von Tempsky was a soldier and amateur artist who is best known for his depictions of the New Zealand Wars.

Level 1.✓ Tick those statements that are an accurate reading of the features of the painting. Be ready to explain your reasons.

1. ☐ Captain Witchell, on his grey steed, is about to swing his sword at the Māori warrior.
2. ☐ The Māori man in front of the tree on the left has bent down to re-load his gun.
3. ☐ Army reinforcements are on their way to assist the two British soldiers.
4. ☐ The painting depicts the moment when Māori rebels were in retreat and were driven into the bush after launching a surprise attack on General Cameron's camp at Nukumaru.
5. ☐ British soldiers are outnumbered by Māori rebels.
6. ☐ The fallen British soldier is in mortal danger.
7. ☐ Von Tempsky follows 19th-century conventions in depicting cavalry with the horse rearing and a heroic fighter taking up a dominant position.
8. ☐ The New Zealand bush with flax and punga trees is accurately portrayed.

Level 2.✓ Tick those statements that are an appropriate interpretation of the painting.

1. ☐ The Māori rebels are depicted as noble, brave fighters.
2. ☐ Von Tempsky aims to suggest that both Māori and the British have equal fighting strength in this encounter.
3. ☐ Von Tempsky was an amateur artist but successfully portrayed the drama of battle.
4. ☐ The painting faithfully conveys the event and is a reliable piece of historical evidence.
5. ☐ The ambush of unsuspecting European soldiers is shown as a cowardly act.
6. ☐ Battle is depicted as a cruel and sordid affair.
7. ☐ Von Tempsky has paid careful attention to Māori appearance and dress.
8. ☐ The battle setting is shown as exotic.

Level 3.✓ Tick those statements that you think Gustavus von Tempsky would have agreed with.

1. ☐ My painting is sufficiently true to be recognisable and sufficiently idealised to suit artistic purposes.
2. ☐ I carefully arranged the figures in the painting to show the superiority of the British forces.
3. ☐ I hoped that my depiction of Māori was 'a fair exposition of that curious and original race of beings'.
4. ☐ I realise my painting is mediocre but I hope that there are a sufficient number of good points in it to permit it to be exhibited and put up for sale.

some of the barriers and difficulties in pedagogical practice and offered some suggestions on how students can purposefully be guided in their investigations of images. The study of visual cultures from times and places far removed from students' experiences offers particular challenges since, in order to read images successfully, students need to be informed about both the historical context and the context in which the image was produced and seen. The more in-depth their contextual understanding, and the more practice students get in using systems of pictorial analysis, the more likely it is that learners will discover layers of meaning in their interpretations of visual imagery:

> It means engaging our students intellectually and emotionally, using their predisposition for the visual to develop their analytical skills and historical knowledge. (Masur, 1998, p. 1423)

References

Barton, K. C. (2005). Primary sources in history: Breaking through the myths. *Phi Delta Kappan, 86*, 745–753.

Bell, L. (1992). *Colonial constructs: European images of Maori 1840–1914*. Auckland: Auckland University Press.

Binney, J., Chaplin, G., & Wallace, C. (1979). *Mihaia: The prophet Rua Kenana and his community at Maungapohatu*. Auckland: Oxford University Press.

Bolvig, A., & Lindley, P. (Eds.). (2003). *History and images: Towards a new iconology*. Turnhout, Belgium: Brepols.

Cooper, R. Wakefield, 'Edward Jerningham—Biography, from the *Dictionary of New Zealand Biography*. Te Ara—The Encyclopedia of New Zealand', updated 1-Sep-10. http://www.TeAra.govt.nz/en/biographies/1w5/1

Coventry, M., Felten, P., Jaffee, D., O'Leary, C., Weis, T., & McGowan, S. (2006). Ways of seeing: Evidence and learning in the history classroom. *Journal of American History, 92*(4), 1371–1402.

Keith, H. (2007). *The big picture: A history of New Zealand art from 1642*. Auckland: Random House.

Masur, L. P. (1998). 'Pictures have now become a necessity': The use of images in American history textbooks. *Journal of American History, 84*(4), 1409–1424.

Ministry of Education. (2007). *The New Zealand curriculum*. Wellington: Learning Media. http://www.nzqa.govt.nz/nqfdocs/ncea-resource/achievements/2012/as91231.pdf

Ormond, B. (2008). *The iconography of visual culture and pedagogical approaches to seeing: Illustrated prints pertaining to religious issues in Early Modern England*. Köln, Germany: Lambert Academic Publishing.

Sharp, I. (2008). *Heaphy*. Auckland: Auckland University Press.

Sinclair, K., & Harrex, W. (1978). *Looking back: A photographic history of New Zealand*. Wellington: Oxford University Press.

Sturken, M., & Cartwright, L. (2001). *Practices of looking: An introduction to visual culture*. Oxford: Oxford University Press.

> "… the only non-negotiable fact about the past is that it is always open to interpretation as it is continually rewritten and redesigned to comply with contemporary issues."
>
> Stuart Foster and Keith Crawford[1]

---

1 S. Foster & K. Crawford. (2006). In S. Foster & K. Crawford (Eds.), *What shall we tell the children?* (pp. 1–23). Greenwich, CT: Information Age Publishing.

CHAPTER 3

Have you asked your students?
Pasifika perspectives on studying history

Christina Reymer

Christina began her undergraduate study in 2006 at the University of Waikato. She has completed a Bachelor of Teaching and Bachelor of Arts, with Honours, in history. For the past 3 years she has taught history at McAuley High School in Otahuhu, South Auckland. Over 90 percent of the students at this school identify themselves as Pacific Islanders. Her daily interactions with Pasifika students motivated her to do research into Pasifika education. Christina has recently completed her Master's in Education which explores Pasifika perspectives on studying history in New Zealand. Her research encourages students to think critically about the nature and purpose of history and to work collaboratively with their teachers to ensure positive learning experiences.

Christina can be contacted at: chr3@waikato.ac.nz

Introduction

Talk with your students, and listen. This would be my advice for any beginning history teacher. Towards the end of last year I began to make a conscious effort to talk to my students as often as possible. As well as talking to them about their life outside of school, I asked them about my classroom practices: when they switched off in class, when they had a lightbulb moment, what I should stop or start doing, what they think about in history, and, importantly, how they think about history. I believe that it is essential for teachers to listen to their students if they are going to form relationships with them that will foster learning in the classroom.

This belief underpins my work. By listening to the experiences of Pasifika students I can develop my pedagogy and critically reflect on my actions in the classroom, in the hope of enhancing the history learning experience. The conversations I have had with Pasifika students have led to the realisation that they experience history through unique cultural lenses, which allows them to understand the constructed and personal nature of historical knowledge.

This chapter discusses my recent classroom-based research on the history curriculum that Pasifika students experience in an integrated, faith-based secondary school in Auckland. My research took place at the end of the 2010 school year and looked at how a cohort of female Year 13 Pasifika students perceived, experienced and understood the history curriculum. This chapter first looks at the use of the term 'Pasifika' in my study and the aims and process of my research. The principles of the Tongan research method 'talanoa' provided the foundation for this research process. This involved a survey and two conversations (talanoa), during which the participants discussed their perspectives, understanding and experiences of studying history in New Zealand.

In order to understand the conversations and experiences of the participants, it is essential to first understand the Pasifika students' identities. Therefore, this chapter also considers the various identities— my own, and the ever-changing identities of the students—at play in this study. In particular, I will look at the way in which the students' identities affect how they experience history, and vice versa. After setting the context of the research, I discuss the students' thinking about history and their perceptions relating to perspectives and interpretation in history.

When considering the projected figures for New Zealand's ethnic composition in 10 years' time, listening to and understanding Pasifika perspectives on studying history in New Zealand becomes even more pertinent. In 2021 the Pasifika population is projected to make up 9.2 percent of the New Zealand population, and in 2040 the majority of students in New Zealand primary schools will be Māori and Pasifika (Wendt-Samu, 2006). Recent statistics on Pasifika students show low levels of achievement, higher levels of suspension and greater rates of unexplained sustained absences from school (Siteine, 2010). The dominant Pākehā culture found in many New Zealand schools is often reflected in traditional methods of formal teaching and a rigid set of values, based on what is considered valid knowledge and how success should be measured. This is in many ways at odds with the cultural values of Pasifika students, and as a result produces many marginalised and unsuccessful learners (Garden, 1998; Nakhid, 2002). With this in mind, the chapter makes an attempt to share with the reader some insights offered by Pasifika students in a Year 13 history class about how they experience and understand history in a New Zealand school's Year 13 history programme.

The decision to use the term 'Pasifika'

This chapter uses the term 'Pasifika' because it is in line with current educational terminology. Many Pacific Island languages translate 'Pacific' as 'Pasifika'. Also, Pasifika researcher Tanya Wendt-Samu notes that "the fact that as a term it 'originated' from us is of no small consequence because being able to define ourselves is an issue of control" (Wendt-Samu, 2006, p. 36). Using 'Pasifika' as a collective term can be problematic, however, because there is a danger that by using such a blanket term researchers will fail to appreciate the diversity the term represents (McFall-McCaffery, 2010; Nakhid, 2002). Wendt-Samu argues that collectivising terms such as 'Pasifika' should not imply homogeneity, but rather should be used in instances "when the common interest of all the island people can be served by collaboration" (Wendt-Samu, 2006, p. 40). Therefore, I use 'Pasifika' to describe and include peoples from many Pacific cultures, while recognising and acknowledging the various traditions and values unique to each cultural group that is represented under the Pasifika umbrella.

The reasons for this history research

This classroom-based history research took place in 2010 in a decile 1 Catholic secondary school with Year 13 students. I was employed as a first-year history teacher at this school, which has a predominantly Pasifika demographic. My involvement with Pasifika students and their communities was a catalyst for further professional development. I began to reflect on how the cultural understandings of the students in my class might influence the way in which they experience the history curriculum. My history research aimed to create an opportunity to listen to the voices of Year 13 Pasifika history students. I wanted to shed light on experiences, issues and attitudes that Pasifika students have when studying history at secondary school. I also wanted this evidence to inform teacher understanding and enhance student learning experiences in history.

At the same time, I hope the Year 13 girls in this study found personal satisfaction from being able to discuss their learning and share with others their perspectives and experiences. This is not to be mistaken as goodwill and intervention, but rather as a way to provide an opportunity to develop the way in which students reflect on and make sense of their learning experiences, especially those related to the study of history.

The classroom-based research approach

I felt that the cross-cultural sensitivities and the complexities of the students' identities involved indicated a mixed-methods approach for the research. The methodology needed to engage the qualitative, interpretive and cultural components of this study. A Tongan research approach, talanoa, encompassed the very cultural and oral aspects that I sought for the methodology of this research. Talanoa is a conversation or personal encounter in which the participants relate their experiences in an informal way, without a rigid framework. This allows more *mo'oni* (pure, real, authentic) information to be available for Pacific research than data derived from other research methods. The talanoa method allows Pasifika students to "identify issues, and then co-create knowledge and solutions for themselves", which in turn links to the aims of my research (Vaioleti, 2006, p. 32). Talanoa is particularly concerned with the relationship between researcher and participant. This was important here, because, as discussed later, my identity located me as both insider and outsider to this research.

In addition to using talanoa, my research also embraced the Samoan concept of *teu le va*, which means to maintain, nurture and cherish the relationship (Anae, 2010). By drawing on Tongan and Samoan concepts for my research, I was able to create a foundation of trust and respect with the participants so that genuine information, stories and experiences were shared. As a history teacher and researcher it was important for me to be faithful to the students' languages and cultures, and the perspectives they shared with me during this research. Selecting a qualitative method meant that a level of interpretation was required on my part, as a researcher and as a teacher, and how I made sense of the students' voice inevitably influenced the conclusions I drew.

The classroom-based research: What actually happened?

The classroom-based research design involved an initial face-to-face meeting with Pasifika students in the Year 13 history class. This was an informal meeting in which I talked to the students about my proposed research and how they had the choice to participate. After this, all consenting students in the class were given a survey, which asked them about their perceptions and experiences of history. Following the survey, these students took part in two group conversations (talanoa), which took place in after-school hours in October 2010. The talanoa were in a relaxed setting with no rigid framework or agenda. Each talanoa lasted approximately 1 hour. Before both conversations the group prayed and shared food. Both prayer and communal meals are common daily acts for the participants in this study, and these rituals helped to create a relaxed, secure and familiar setting for the students.

During the first talanoa we referred back to the survey responses and discussed them in a more informal and collaborative way. As the researcher I was listening for moments in which students offered their own perspectives and insights into their experiences of studying history in New Zealand. I was interested in how students connected with or made sense of the history they were studying.

I then analysed the data that arose from the conversation using a thematic approach. In order to improve the validity and credibility of the conclusions drawn from my research, a follow-up talanoa was held with willing participants. This allowed students to reflect on my initial interpretations of the data collected from the group conversation, and to further elaborate on and discuss their meaning. Many of these themes were co-constructed by the participants during the talanoa.

My identities in the history research: Outsider and insider

I believe that every piece of research is both limited and improved by the identities involved in the process, not least by the identity of the researcher. Who I *feel* I am has strongly influenced this study and its conclusions. Although this study is essentially about the Year 13 Pasifika history students at my school, I am unavoidably interwoven in the discussions and the conclusions and therefore my identity also needs to be considered. Identity theorist James Cote (1996) has argued that our identities develop as a result of our place in contemporary society, our family, our culture, and the institutions we operate in. My family's experiences, culture and interactions with others contribute to my negotiated and ever-changing identity, which underpins my educational experiences.

As the researcher in this study I asked many of the questions and facilitated many of the conversations. I was also the teacher: I was part of the school community of these participants and I shared in their learning experiences. My identity therefore positions me as both an insider and an outsider in this research, and there are strengths and limitations in each instance (Schroenberger, 1992; Smith, 1999). As a teacher I remain firmly within the researched community. However, as a person without a Pasifika identity and a master's student focused on a particular research context, my interpretation and views of the conversations re-position me in many ways as an outsider. This dual role is significant because it may influence the depth of information shared and perhaps withheld from me, but also how I interpret the language and ideas expressed in the conversations I had with these students. Our gender, class, race, nationality, politics, history and experience shape our research and our interpretations of the world, however much we deny it (Schroenberger, 1992). The task is not to do away with these things, but to acknowledge and learn from them.

The identities of the students in this classroom-based research

Our students' identities affect their classroom and educational experiences. The understandings students bring with them into the classroom create the lens through which they experience their history education. Therefore, attempting to understand the identities of Pasifika students in this research is an essential part of this chapter. Pasifika students construct their identities as a result of participation and experiences in their private, cultural and public communities as Pasifika. I believe that as these students change between their daily environments, such as individual classrooms, school, home and church, the decision on when to be or not to be Pasifika is a ground often negotiated. I use the term 'be' because our identity is a fluid state of being that changes and adapts to different environments and situations (Gee, 2000), and this appears to be particularly true of the Pasifika students.

Researchers in the field of Pasifika education, such as Camille Nakhid (2002) and Alexis Siteine, (2010), contend that the role of identity, as it is constructed *by* the individual and *for* the individual, is central to the understanding, experience and achievement of Pasifika students. The girls in this study had a repertoire of identities to choose from in order to fit the environment they found themselves in. This highlights the importance of the fluidity of the participants' identities, which allows them to select which aspects of their identities are expressed in different places and at different times. Sometimes it seemed as if these students compromised or put aside their Pasifika identity in order to fit in with the values the school and society had deemed important, such as those relating to learning, knowledge and success. I was made aware of this during the talanoa, when the Pasifika students began to talk about their own perceptions of the past and history from a Pasifika perspective. This sharing revealed a unique sense of history inside all the students, and it is through this way of knowing that they experience history in the classroom.

Most of the Pasifika students at my school have time-consuming commitments to their religious and cultural groups. The decision to be an active participant of these groups often arises from an expectation and pressure from parents and their communities. From my experiences with Pasifika students, I believe that their cultural and religious involvement has important implications for the identity formation of Pasifika learners, because it means they adopt a life course that revolves around a predetermined set of commitments and beliefs that have been prioritised for them by their parents, elders in the community or religious leaders. As discussed in the next section, this acceptance of beliefs and ways of being creates a unique challenge for history teachers.

Despite a seemingly stable commitment to culture and religion, the participants in this study sometimes opted out of their cultural identity as a way to adapt to the environment they found themselves in. Pasifika students at school are called "plastic" (not *really* Pasifika) by their peers if they achieve highly academically. One of my students once said to me about another student, "She is Palagi-as in class, she always asks questions". This suggests that students see being Pasifika as incompatible with academic pursuits and perhaps reflects an awareness of the deficit theorising that exists in relation to Pasifika students.

Pasifika youth have been portrayed in educational discussions and government policy as low achieving and of low socioeconomic status (Hernandez Sheets, 2005; Nakhid, 2002; Portes, 2005). Statistics show them to be disadvantaged in various aspects of education, such as achievement, suspensions and unexplained absences from school (Siteine, 2010). With these markers continuing to define the Pasifika student identity, it is no wonder that many Pasifika students shed allegiances to the Pasifika culture the minute they walk through the school gate in order to fit in with the identity and culture of the school. The dominant Pākehā culture found in many New Zealand schools is in many ways at odds with the cultural values of the students in my research. As a result, the education system has the potential to marginalise learners and compromise success (Garden, 1998; Hill, 1994). If these students do not identify with the culture of the classroom, they may become disengaged and underachieve, thus reinforcing the stereotype of Pasifika students.

How studying history contributes to the identity formation of Pasifika students

The cultural and religious understanding that many Pasifika students share has important implications for history teachers. In the Samoan culture, to question authority and tradition is seen as inappropriate and as challenging fa'asamoa (traditional Samoan knowledge). As a result, Pasifika students are often taught to listen and obey without questioning (Fletcher, Parkhill, Fa'afoi, Taleni, & O'Regan, 2009; Tiatia, 1998). In the history classroom these same students are being asked to argue with historical narratives, interpret the past, have divergent viewpoints, and question widely accepted "truths". As Tiatia (1998) points out, this could be problematic for Pasifika learners because it requires them to move themselves mentally from the identities and role they have in their family, traditional church and culture. Engagement with history could be in many ways contrary to their cultural way of being.

However, students may also come to better understand their identity as a result of the topics studied in history. Many participants in this study had been given the opportunity to study the Mau movement as part of the classroom curriculum. Mau was a non-violent movement in Samoa that began in the early 1900s to work for independence from colonial rule. For the Samoan students in this study, learning about the Mau movement helped to define and clarify their identities. Grace, one of the research participants commented:

> Knowing that my Granddad was half German. I never knew how that happened. Like, how did the Germans get to Samoa? ... And when I studied the Mau movement I realised it was [because] Germany had occupied it. And it made **me** ... realise, maybe this is why I am who I am. Maybe my ancestors were part of the troops that had occupied Samoa ... I don't know, it just makes me understand more about my past, and my culture.

In the extract above, Grace allows us to see how the incorporation of the Mau movement into the classroom history curriculum gave her a greater understanding of who she is. However, the language Grace uses, "maybe this is why" and "I don't know", indicates that her conceptions of her identity are in the process of being formed. Another student, Sena, explained that before studying the Mau movement her siblings called her "plastic", a term Pasifika youth also use to describe someone who is not able to speak the native language. Sena had internalised being plastic as part of her identity and accepted it. After studying the Mau movement, she realised that being able to speak Samoan is not the single determining criterion of being a true Samoan:

> It was interesting, because when I speak Samoan, I am so not fluent ... [my siblings] call me plastic, and learning about Samoa ... the Mau movement ... I found it cool as, cos it was about where my mum, and my ancestors and all them came from. I liked it. I'm not plastic now!

For Sena, studying the history of the Mau movement allowed her to find a sense of belonging and acceptance of her Samoan identity despite being New Zealand born and a predominantly English speaker. This aligns with the work of Wendt-Samu, who contends that many Pasifika students have a

> notion of a shared identity where the New Zealand born or New Zealand raised Pacific Islander wishes to be multiethnic or bicultural on their own terms. This is a conscious and deliberate construction which means it is ok not to be fluent in the language and protocols. (2006, p. 40)

The classroom-based research reveals a Pasifika sense of history

As the second talanoa was coming to an end, I took the opportunity to ask the girls a final question: "What unique concepts or understandings about the past and history are there in your culture?" Without hesitation a Samoan student, Laine, answered, "respect". Her culture, but more importantly the past attached to her culture, came with traditions, actions and even a unique distinction in language that was centred around the concept of respect. Her ancestors had established rules and formalities relating to hierarchy and authority, along with cultural protocols, which in her opinion were founded on the principle of respect. These formalities, through repetition over the years, had become a way of acknowledging the past. For this student, respect had become a central concept of history. This idea was supported by the group, and Grace, also Samoan, elaborated that there was a "specialness" about studying the past because:

> it still happens today, our parents teach us … in our culture, what they did back in the day … and they still do that, but only because they did it back in the day. So we will do it when we grow up, you can never get rid of it, it will always stay with us.

The cultural understanding of the students in this study determined how they viewed history. The participants agreed that history for them was about stories, and that the study of history was just a continuation of learning stories and traditions—from their own past and from the past of others. The students in this study expressed the idea that learning history was not just about respect, but that historical knowledge was "a special kind of knowledge" that came with an obligation to "share it", "tell your kids" and "keep doing it". For these students, the deliberate repetition of the past was an inherent part of being themselves.

As the students talked about their own cultural understanding of the past they revealed a personal sense of history. This personal history was an historical consciousness that was not learned but rather a product of the student's life interactions and experiences. Learning history was synonymous with the past, the deeds of ancestors and tradition. The insight provided at this point in the talanoa is explained by the work of Wendt-Samu (2010), who writes that "amongst Pasifika learners are unique and institutionalised ways of knowing and relating to the world. What is needed is tailor-made contextualised teaching" (p. 8). This personal sense of history has important implications for teachers, because it is through this cultural lens of understanding and historical consciousness that students experience history in the classroom (Seixas, 2004). The responses of the research participants led me to reflect that the students in my history class are also likely to have their own personal sense of history. This understanding of the past is part of their identity. Therefore, if I am to ensure my students' identities are "recognised and heard" in the classroom, as the Ministry of Education requires (2007, p. 9), I need to make sure that this internalised personal history of my students, which is so central to their identities, is validated as a legitimate understanding of history.

Having a personal sense of history does not imply that students cannot connect with or find relevance in other topics studied in history, however. Indeed, the participants of this study proved this was not the case. Students have an "historical consciousness" that helps them to personally connect with history and see the big picture (Hunter & Farthing, 2007; Seixas, 2004). My students felt they would find enjoyment and relevance learning about World Wars I and II, the rise and fall of empires, the cultural history of Japan and major world movements, and can connect with these contexts in a very personal way through their own lens of understanding. During the talanoa, Laine commented that she wanted to learn about Iraq and Turkey. When her peers laughed she said:

> I'm serious it would be interesting—they have, like, their own traditions and stuff, there [are] heaps of groups out there that still carry on their traditions and we can relate it to our culture, how we still carry on our traditions.

This reflects the findings of Brophy and Alleman (2005, cited in Aitken & Sinnema, 2008, p. 64), who argue that by focusing on "cultural universals" (for instance traditions, languages and rituals), we provide a means of keeping content close to the students' life experiences. The concept of tradition can be seen as a cultural universal. All cultures have their own unique set of traditions, and although these traditions differ markedly across the cultures of the world, the presence of traditions in all cultures can help connect students with the historical context being studied. Laine's comments show that she was able to find relevance in studying Turkish history because she could draw comparisons between their rich cultural traditions and her own traditions from Samoan culture. In my research the students have said that as a result of studying history they can now make these connections themselves. Furthermore, the content does not have to be explicitly relevant to them, because they can find personal connections from the themes.

The students discuss the role of perspectives and interpretation in history

My research has shown that students are able to identify the type of thinking that is required when studying history. The participants also discussed the various understandings they have of the history curriculum. The following conversation highlights the complex way in which Pasifika students engage with historical knowledge and historical narratives.

Researcher: What type of thinking do you need in history?
Tee: No thinking [only half joking!].
[The laughter subsides.]
Trish: You have to think critically …
Grace: Yeah, you have to think from the historical point of view.
Laine: Can you trust this? Is this what actually happened? Is there enough evidence to support it? … Is it reliable?
Sera: It makes you think beyond what you usually do … It pushes the boundaries … It doesn't just limit you to think about that situation. You need to think about its many points of view …
Laine: Yeah, you have to think about if there is anything else that has to do with it, like was it connected to anything else.

This moment in the talanoa reinforced for me some of the observations I have made from my own experiences in the history classroom. Despite the challenge of fa'asamoa, I am beginning to see, through the classroom interactions I have with Pasifika students, a very slow but definite change in the students' ability to challenge and contest historical claims. History educators Keith Barton and Linda Levstik (2003) contend that

> Students should learn how such stories are developed in the first place … They should understand the relationship between historical evidence and the construction of accounts … that the same evidence can lead to divergent interpretations. (p. 358)

It is encouraging to hear in the conversations on perspectives and interpretation that the participants in my study seemed to have developed an understanding of history that Barton and Levstik (2003) deem important in a good history student. When asked about the nature of perspectives and interpretation in history, the group came up with heartening responses:

Laine: You can have different interpretations because as [Mr X] was saying he thinks [the Treaty] was well intentioned, just a misunderstanding, but then others may say this was on purpose!

Trish: There may be one story but then there [are] always different sides and points of view to the story.

These selected quotes demonstrate that the Pasifika students in this study have a sense that history is contested. At one point in the talanoa we discussed how historians have different explanations of how events of the past happened and how they use historical sources to support their explanation. At this point Laine said:

> I like to do that, I can do that … I like maths cos I like solving stuff. I like history cos it's like I'm a problem solver. You have to think about other stuff [in the past] and how it came about to this [the event studied]. It is like you are given a situation … and then some problems … and you need to find the right problem to go with the answer.

In these responses Laine is acknowledging that there are several possible explanations for how and why an event in history occurred. Throughout the talanoa the participants showed that thinking about history requires an understanding of the need for interpretation and the consideration of multiple perspectives. Pasifika students recognised that the very nature of history meant that they could actively construct their own understanding of the past, and they longed for more opportunity to do this in the history classroom.

Conclusion: What all this tells history teachers

If we are to ensure that our students' identities are "recognised and heard", then we need to learn about, acknowledge and validate the cultural understandings that students bring with them to the classroom. Pasifika students, like all students, have a unique sense of the past. It is through this lens of understanding that students experience history. In addition to understanding their students' identities, teachers can help students to connect with different historical contexts by focusing on cultural universals in the history topics taught. This may also help to teach students how to look for and make these connections themselves.

Schools and teachers also need to consider how traditional approaches to education may present a challenge for students whose cultural ways of being may be at odds with what is considered attractive qualities of a 21st century learner. Teachers need to make conscious efforts to avoid the deficit theorising that occurs around Pasifika students. If real change is to occur, Pasifika students cannot be defined by underachievement and low socioeconomic status. Instead, we need to recognise that students can understand the complex nature of historical knowledge through a lens of their own cultural understanding. The students in this research understood the role of interpretation and perspectives in history. They saw the process of constructing history not as an academic pursuit exclusive to historians, but rather as an activity they too were able to partake in. They longed for opportunities to do this in the history classroom.

Pasifika students have a unique perspective and understanding of history, and this in turn engages them in their learning. As usual, the students say it best: "People think history is boring because they don't understand it, they don't get it ... But when *you* take it, *you* come to understand it. When *you* are understanding something, *you* like it!"

Afterword

This chapter is informed by my master's research. The research is supervised by Philippa Hunter, senior lecturer in social sciences and curriculum and policy studies in education at the University of Waikato.

References

Aitken, G., & Sinnema, C. (2008). *Effective pedagogy in social sciences/Tikanga ā iwi: Best evidence synthesis iteration [BES]*. Wellington: Ministry of Education.

Anae, M. (2010). Research for better Pacific schooling in New Zealand: Teu le va: A Samoan perspective. *Mai Review, 1*. Retrieved 5 May 2010 from http://review.mai.ac.nz/index.php/MR/article/view/298/395

Barton, K. C., & Levstik, L. S. (2003). Why don't more history teachers engage students in interpretation? *Social Education, 67*(6), 358-362.

Cote, J. E. (1996). Sociological perspectives on identify formation: The culture-identity link and identity capital. *Journal of Adolescence, 19*, 417-428.

Fletcher, J., Parkhill, F., Fa'afoi, A., Teleni, L. T., & O'Regan, B. (2009). Pasifika students: Teachers and parents voice their perceptions of what provides supports and barriers to Pasifika students' achievement in literacy and learning. *Teacher and Teacher Education, 25*, 24-33.

Garden, R. A. (Ed.). (1998). *Mathematics and science literacy in the final year of schooling: Results from New Zealand's participation in the third international mathematics and science study*. Wellington: Ministry of Education.

Gee, J. P. (2000). Identity as an analytic lens for research in education. *Review of research in education, 25*(1), 99-125.

Hernandez Sheets, R. (2005). *Diversity pedagogy: Examining the role of culture in the teaching-learning process*. Boston, MA: Allyn & Bacon.

Hill, B. V. (1994). *Teaching secondary social studies in a multicultural society*. Melbourne, VIC: Longman Cheshire.

Hunter, P., & Farthing, B. (2007). Connecting learners with their pasts as a way into history. set: *Research Information for Teachers, 1*, 21-26.

McFall-McCaffery, J. (2010). Getting started with Pacific research: Finding resources and information on Pacific research models and methodologies. *Mai Review, 1*. Retrieved 5 May 2010 from http://ojs.review.mai.ac.nz/index.php/MR/article/view/332/367

Ministry of Education. (2007). *The New Zealand curriculum*. Wellington: Learning Media.

Ministry of Social Development. (2010). *Ethnic composition of the population*. Retrieved 1 August 2011 from http://socialreport.msd.govt.nz/people/ethnic-composition-population.html.

Nakhid, C. (2002). *Who do you say I am?—Explaining the marginalized status of Pasifika students' academic achievement by examining the conflict between institutional perceptions and the 'identifying process'*. Paper presented at the Comparative and International Education Society Conference. Retrieved 5 May 2010 from http://www.eric.ed.gov/contentdelivery/servlet/ERICServlet?accno=ED470512

Portes, P. R. (2005). *Dismantling educational inequality: A cultural-historical approach to closing the achievement gap*. New York, NY: Peter Lang.

Schroenberger, E. (1992). Self criticism and self awareness in research. *Professional Geographer, 44*(2), 215–218.

Seixas, P. (2004). Introduction. In P. Seixas (Ed.), *Theorising historical consciousness* (pp. 1–20). Toronto, ON: Toronto University Press.

Siteine, A. (2010). The allocation of Pasifika identity in the New Zealand classrooms. *Mai Review, 1*. Retrieved 5 May 2010 from http://ojs.review.mai.ac.nz/index.php/MR/article/view/301/383

Smith, L. T. (1999). *Decolonizing methodologies: Research and indigenous peoples*. Dunedin, London, New York: University of Otago/Zed Books.

Tiatia, J. (1998). *Caught between cultures: A New Zealand-born Pacific Island perspective*. Auckland: Christian Research Association.

Vaioleti, T. M. (2006). Talanoa research methodology: A developing position on Pacific research. *Waikato Journal of Education, 12*, 21–34.

Wendt-Samu, T. (2006). The 'Pasifika umbrella' and quality teaching: Understanding and responding to the diverse realities within. *Waikato Journal of Education, 12*, 35–49.

Wendt-Samu, T. (2010). Pacific education: An Oceanic perspective. *Mai Review, 1*, 1–14. Retrieved 5 May 2010 from http://ojs.review.mai.ac.nz/index.php/MR/article/view/311/379

CHAPTER 4

Museums and historical literacy: Unpacking the narratives of war and nationhood

BRONWYN HOULISTON

> Before becoming a teacher, Bronwyn completed a Master of Arts in Museums and Cultural Heritage through the History Department at the University of Auckland. After a brief stint as a parliamentary executive assistant and a foray into the world of advertising, Bronwyn returned to the University of Auckland in 2009 to undertake a graduate diploma in secondary school teaching. Bronwyn is now very happily in her third year of teaching history and social studies at McAuley High School in Otahuhu, Auckland.
>
> Bronwyn can be contacted at: bhouliston@mcauleyhigh.school.nz

Introduction

As history teachers we encourage students to critically engage with historical sources, prompting them to consider issues of bias, perspective and selection of evidence. Although we are aware of the need to develop the historical literacy of our students in the classroom, often when we take students on educational experiences outside the classroom this focus is overlooked. Ironically, it is during educational experiences outside the classroom such as trips to museums, where history has been constructed or selected for students, that the historical literacy of our students assumes the most value and provides them with the opportunity to critically engage with public history.

The Ministry of Education's desire to encourage students to become active participants in society sits comfortably with international developments concerning the teaching and learning of the social sciences, and history in particular (Ministry of Education, 2009). Taylor and Young (2003, p. 5) argue that "historical literacy" rather than "the mere recall of historical facts" should be the focus of effective historical pedagogy. Historical literacy in this context is defined as "a systematic process, with particular sets of skills, attitudes and conceptual understandings that mediates and develops historical consciousness". Within the "index of historical literacy" outlined by Taylor and Young (p. 33) sits the element of "contention and contestability", where students are encouraged to engage with public historical discussion and debate. In this chapter I analyse the popular *Scars on the Heart* exhibition at the Auckland War Memorial Museum to illustrate how museum exhibitions are constructed notions of history. I use this analysis to argue that museum exhibitions, and their narratives in particular, provide a vehicle through which students can develop this element of their historical literacy.

Fiona McLean (1998) argues that museums select and interpret evidence for their audience, yet students and the general public alike are often not trained to look for that selection or to ask, 'Who has been left out?' This chapter will explore the different ways we can support students to recognise areas of contention and contestability in public history. Using a permanent exhibition at one of our largest museums as a case study, I will discuss the common challenges students (and the public) encounter at museum exhibitions and suggest learning experiences that can provide students (and teachers) with the tools to think like a historian outside the classroom.

The museum and the construction of identity

Museums are sites of interaction between the public and history. They are "major communicators to the public about the past" (Jordanova, 2000). That "past", however, is loaded with political and social assumptions. Museums are regularly censured for acting as "emotional and social refuges where the past is rearranged to suit the needs of the moment"

(Kavanagh, 1990). However, while historians have become increasingly aware of how they construct historical narratives and of the absence of fixed truths, museums and curators have been slower to recognise their role in the construction of historical knowledge (Bunch, 1992). This role has keen implications for history teachers who encourage their students to use the museum exhibition as a resource, or to see it as a medium for the communication of historical ideas.

The role of the museum in the construction of a national identity becomes especially pertinent when our two largest museums (Te Papa Tongarewa and the Auckland War Memorial Museum) are preoccupied with telling the story of the nation or the story of the nation at war, which are worryingly perceived by many as one and the same. Significant government and council investment in exhibitions that tell the nation's story have had a considerable impact on the historical narrative constructed and typically these exhibitions are designed to have wide public appeal. Although history is increasingly recognised by historians and curators as contested terrain, some members of the public would prefer museums to provide them with a clear narrative that will reinforce what they believe to be their national identity. This preference, however, is often in direct conflict with a wider desire to introduce the public to problematised histories.

Museums are in many ways more engaging and powerful than textbooks. They are designed to entertain and engage an audience, providing 'educational entertainment'. While offering an enjoyable experience for a family outing, using 'the nation' as an explanatory framework for the construction of a history exhibition is likely to inhibit the ability of a museum to exhibit a nuanced view of the past. Our desire to be entertained can lead to complete buy-in to an exhibition, and result in the passive consumption of the exhibition narrative in a similar way that audiences might enjoy a blockbuster film: we go along for the ride, wanting to be entertained and excited. It therefore becomes increasingly important that teachers enter into conversations with their students about the constructed nature of historical knowledge prior to visiting a museum or public history exhibition. There are learning experiences we can facilitate in the classroom to prepare students before visiting museum exhibitions and prompt them to look beyond the label.

Exhibiting the Pākehā warrior: *Scars on the Heart*

The Auckland War Memorial Museum is perhaps best known for its long-term permanent exhibition *Scars on the Heart*. The museum offers a range of educational opportunities for teachers and students related to the exhibition, while the current history curriculum's focus on the two world wars, along with the supporting educational resources provided for the exhibits, suggests that the exhibition is a well-utilised educational resource.

Scott Worthy (2001) argues that memorials and the commemoration of war provide an important foundation for the construction of a "New Zealand identity". General and military histories have constructed an archetypal male New Zealand character that has subsequently come to define New Zealand society as a whole. Consequently, the belief that New Zealand's nationhood was "established by the performance of its men at war" constitutes the dominant framework employed by many historians writing New Zealand's military and general history (Phillips, 1989, p. 91). *Scars on the Heart* closely mirrors the extant historiography: it emphasises war as the dominant framework through which national identity can be discerned. In doing so, the exhibition also highlights the development of distinct national characteristics: racial harmony, the nation itself being established through the New Zealand and South African Wars and the unique characteristics of New Zealand soldiers—and therefore New Zealand society—being crystallised and solidified in both world wars. However, just as *Scars on the Heart* mirrors New Zealand's written military history, it also reflects the silences inherent in that history. As a consequence, dissenting viewpoints are overwhelmingly marginalised in the exhibition in favour of a narrative that emphasises the seamless development of a unified nation: on-going racial conflict since the New Zealand Wars threatens a discourse of racial unity and is thus obscured, while conscientious objectors to World War I challenge the consensus that underpinned New Zealand's involvement in the Great War and are consequently marginalised.

Giving consideration to the broader picture, students need to consider the purpose of a museum itself. As a familiar part of the cultural landscape, museums, like the memorials and heritage sites highlighted by Harcourt, Fountain and Sheehan (2011), are often perceived as benign social institutions. However, Peter Gibbons' cultural colonisation thesis clearly outlines the extent to which museums have been a vehicle for the "imposition and extension of European power in New Zealand" (1998, p. 38). The process of selection which the museum engages in to choose objects, quotes and even the topic they will display is not accessible to the visitor. Like the memorials described by Harcourt et al. (2011), the museum also defines what is significant to New Zealanders, using the nation as an explanatory framework. Asking students to explore the purpose of a museum opens the door to conversations regarding the role of the museum in the construction of identity and the imagined community (Prior, 2002). Once the constructed nature of the museum is introduced to students, the focus can be narrowed and students can begin to engage with problematising the museum and historical knowledge itself.

Looking beyond the label: Unpacking history

The role of Māori in New Zealand's history at war in *Scars on the Heart* offers students an opportunity to explore problematised histories. *Scars on the Heart* introduces the museum audience to New Zealand at war through a series of conflicts that took place during the 1840s and 1860s on New Zealand soil. The New Zealand Wars have occupied an uneasy position in the historiography of New Zealand at war, and are dominated by misconceptions designed to accommodate an established mythology. By beginning the visitor's journey with the New Zealand Wars, the exhibition makes sense not only chronologically, but in terms of the exhibition's overarching goal—in order to show the growth of the nation through war, *Scars on the Heart* needs to first establish New Zealand as a nation itself.

The New Zealand Wars gallery reflects recent developments in historiography, beginning with the name of the exhibition, and including highlighting Māori success in battle (Gate Pa) and acknowledging ongoing conflict over land confiscations in the years after the war and a reticent attitude towards the wars among the wider public. However, overwhelmingly, *Scars on the Heart* mirrors much of the established historiography. Conflict is acknowledged in exhibition labels and the accompanying video, but it promotes the idea that the situation in New Zealand after the wars was comparable to the words said at Waitangi:

"Now we are one people". The belief that the New Zealand Wars provided a base for harmonious race relations dominates interpretations of Māori participation at war throughout *Scars on the Heart*. Māori involvement in the South African War, 1899–1902, is characterised by a willingness to fight on behalf of the Empire, even though imperial sensibilities prevented them from doing so. In World War I we see racial tensions dissolved on the battlefield as "Maori and Pakeha fought together as 'brothers in arms'" (Gregory, 1999, p. 21). Māori success in war easily fits the harmonious race relations mythology, incorporating Māori achievement while solidifying the perception of a racially unified New Zealand.

Unpacking historical narratives can be difficult without developed prior knowledge. Developing a series of questions, ideally in concert with students, can form the basis of this unpacking. Selecting a theme students can explore can provide them with a critical lens through which to view the exhibition. Possible questions students could consider when unpacking this exhibition, and the role of Māori within it, could include:

- What objects have been selected to represent Māori and Pākehā perspectives?
- What are Māori shown to be doing in the exhibition?
- What are Pākehā shown to be doing in the exhibition?
- What language is used to describe the actions/perspectives of Māori and/or Pākehā (for example, passive or active words)?
- What language is used to describe the relationship between Māori and Pākehā?
- What language has been used by the curators to represent the historical significance of the exhibition?
- How could this exhibition have been created differently?

Using these questions to structure their analysis of the exhibition narrative will serve to prompt students to consider issues of bias, perspective and the selection of evidence made by the curator on behalf of the audience.

Constructing the past ourselves: A teaching and learning activity

Asking students to critically engage with exhibition narrative goes beyond encouraging them to merely identify who or what is missing. Many exhibits include a degree of conflict in the exhibition narrative, but the treatment of that conflict can also raise a number of issues students should be encouraged to consider.

The marginalisation of contested perspectives in favour of content that fits comfortably with the national narrative is never more evident than in the *Scars on the Heart*'s treatment of the war in Vietnam. The exhibit includes a display entitled *Kiwis in Asia: Conflict in Vietnam, Malaya and Borneo*. The role of the Vietnam War in the development of the nation, unlike World Wars I and II, is much less clear and open to debate. Comprising a relatively small display, partially obscured by a wall, the war in Vietnam takes precedence over conflict in Malaya and Borneo throughout the exhibit's narrative. The ambiguous position the war has traditionally occupied in the national consciousness stems directly from unprecedented public opposition against New Zealand's involvement in the conflict. The exhibition deals with this ambiguity by focusing on those parts of the conflict that sit more comfortably within New Zealand's national identity. The exhibit's abstract does not include a description of conflicts after 1945, including New Zealand's involvement in Malaya, Borneo and Vietnam. Such an omission seems to imply that these conflicts are considered peripheral to the development of New Zealand's sense of national identity.

Traditionally painted as the "reluctant ally" in order to distance New Zealand from its role in the conflict, this sentiment is mirrored in *Kiwis in Asia* through the introductory subheading 'Reluctantly into Vietnam'. A lack of personal objects from the war (in contrast to the other displays in *Scars on the Heart*) and a wall devoted to the anti-war movement consolidates this uncertain position. The emphasis placed on the anti-war movement is significant and provides students with an example of how conflict can be interpreted so that it sits comfortably within the national narrative. By linking the protest movement to New Zealand's identity, the anti-war movement is given national characteristics, and comes to represent a wider struggle against social injustice and the beginnings of a new identity for New Zealanders, solidified by later protests against apartheid and nuclear testing. Consequently, those who supported the war, and their justification for that support, have been marginalised from the historiography and exhibition narrative. While the anti-war movement is dominated by conflict, it is subsumed into the national narrative, eventually unifying New Zealanders under the banner of international conflict.

Scars on the Heart has served as a useful case study for the purposes of this chapter, but the Auckland War Memorial Museum is not alone in championing the dominant master narrative. Te Papa's *Slice of Heaven* is a recent example of a long-term exhibition whose considerable expense requires justification in terms of public appeal. Focused on 20th century New Zealand history, *Slice of Heaven* examines what has "united and divided us, and shaped our lives today". It supposedly examines the roles of conflict within the construction of the nation's identity, but conflict also acts as a unifying force in *Slice of Heaven*. Taking up where *Scars on the Heart* finishes off, *Slice of Heaven* identifies conflict over the Springbok tour, the women's movement and gay rights as unifying experiences which resulted in a more "inclusive" New Zealand, whereby "'they' had become 'us'". *Slice of Heaven* demonstrates to students that even when including conflict within an exhibition dialogue, it is still possible to do so comfortably within the master narrative. As Barton and Levstik (2004, p. 137) acknowledge, "no historical account can be comprehensive": constructing historical narratives requires the selection of different perspectives. However, students and museums alike are increasingly asked to explore a range of perspectives, including those previously marginalised. This does not necessarily mean that these divergent perspectives are always given as much weight as the dominant narrative. Barton and Levstik (2004, p. 137) make the point that historians at times "still treat[ed] them [marginalised perspectives] less as the agents of history than as the objects of manipulation by those in power".

Using the museum exhibit in the classroom to problematise history

The museum exhibit is no longer only found outside of the classroom: students are often asked to construct museum exhibits in order to communicate historical information for assessment. A current Level 3 internal assessment resource available for use on tki.org.nz asks students to prepare a submission to a fictitious "Museum Director seeking support for the Museum to mount a display on one of the important battles or campaigns of World War Two" (Ministry of Education, 2009, pp. 3-4). Included in this submission is a memo "which develops a convincing argument about why this battle would be of interest or value to visitors to the Museum" (p. 4). Tasks such as these offer students the opportunity to problematise history in order to explore issues such as historical significance and perspective. However, if a student's initial introduction to the medium of a museum exhibit is through the assessment task itself, they will lack the understanding required to make full use of this opportunity and develop this area of their historical literacy.

Using museum exhibits as teaching and learning experiences within the classroom provides teachers with the opportunity to introduce the contested nature of such exhibits to students, while also offering them the chance to think and act like a historian, engaging with and interpreting a wide range of primary sources. Jennifer Frost (2000, p. 363) discusses her attempt to merge a more "inclusive history with a more interactive classroom" through the use of museum exhibits as teaching and learning experiences in tertiary education. Using Irish immigrant women as a case study, Frost provides students with 10 images, including drawings, photographs and cartoons. Students "must select their images, order them, and on their coversheet explain their choices and sequence, they must also give their exhibit a title" (p. 364). Allowing students to select and interpret evidence opens a dialogue among students about the constructed nature of history. Frost encourages students to compare and contrast the different exhibits created by the class, providing them with the opportunity to "see that all historians select, order, and interpret evidence to make an argument" (pp. 364-365).

This teaching and learning experience could easily be translated to secondary classrooms. The teacher could provide students with visuals, written sources (such as excerpts from oral histories) or objects from a range of perspectives and ask them to select and interpret the sources. While justifying their selection and ordering of the items in their exhibit, students could also write labels for each object, prompting them to consider the limited nature of exhibition labels and to make choices about the type of language used and the information included or excluded.

Once their exhibits have been constructed, there is the opportunity for students to critically engage with museum narratives. Students could present their exhibits alongside each other and develop a range of questions through which they can unpack the exhibit and look for issues of contention and contestability. This activity provides students with an opportunity to construct the past and see that not only is it constructed, it is also often contested. Making links between the exhibits they have created and those they see presented in public museums is the next step in developing and applying this historical literacy to a wider context. By providing students with the tools to unpack the use of conflict in exhibitions which chart the development of the nation, they can become aware of the potential pitfalls associated with treating museum exhibitions as depositories of knowledge, and can learn instead to treat them as the constructed 'text' they are.

Identifying areas of contestation and contestability as teachers

As teachers we must ask ourselves the same questions we pose for students and critically evaluate the educational resources supplied to us, given that the process of selection regarding what is taught to students—or provided for teachers—is not always clear. For example, the *Scars on the Heart* teacher resource quickly moves from the conclusion of World War II in the Pacific to *Fighting under the Blue Beret*, an examination of New Zealand's involvement in the United Nations, silencing New Zealand's involvement in the Vietnam War while reinforcing the mythology of "an outward-looking and cooperative nation, coexisting peacefully in the Pacific and beyond" (Auckland War Memorial Museum, n.d.; Taylor & Young, 2003). This critical evaluation can also extend to our own units and the process by which we select and interpret history for our students. For example, as a result of the established historiographical tradition, the Year 11 unit 'The origins of the Second World War', and the texts that support it, have often encouraged a Eurocentric interpretation whereby the "path to destruction" is presented as linear, and at times inevitable (Mills, 1985). Which histories are silenced merely because we have followed established units of work based on unchallenged assumptions? Perhaps the next step is to engage students in critiquing not only the history they are presented with outside the classroom in museums and war memorials, but also the history they are presented with by us.

Conclusion

Museum exhibits provide a vehicle through which students can develop their historical literacy. Museums select objects that are 'worthy' of preservation and display. They contextualise artefacts, construct explicit or implicit narratives, and offer the public a visual interpretation of the past. Kavanagh (1990, p. 127) argues that the purpose of a history exhibition is to "open up a dialogue about the past" rather than provide fixed interpretations or "essential historical truths". While museums increasingly acknowledge the role they play in shaping the public's understanding of history (Schlereth, 1992), effective history pedagogy, both inside and outside the classroom, can provide students with the framework required to actively engage with and problematise history. This means not only taking students to the museum, but also bringing the museum into the classroom to better understand the process of selection and interpretation embarked upon by historians and curators when constructing historical knowledge.

The teaching and learning experiences in this chapter are suggestions that could easily be adapted to meet the needs of a variety of classrooms. By doing history and constructing their own museum exhibits through a process of selection and interpretation, students are actively participating in the disciplinary aspects of history and will be better placed to problematise the past, not only as presented in museum exhibits but also in government history publications and online media. Empowering students not only to think like a historian but also to act like one creates better-informed citizens and increases the relevance of history, allowing students to identify examples in everyday life where aspects of our history have been selected and interpreted for us.

References

Auckland War Memorial Museum. (n.d.). *Scars on the Heart Resource Book for Teachers*. Retrieved 10 October 2011 from http://www.aucklandmuseum.com/site_resources/library/Education/Teachers_Guide/Teacher_Resources_Library/War_Memorial/ScarsOnTheHeart.pdf

Barton, K., & Levstik, L.S. (2004). *Teaching history for the common good*. Hillsdale, NJ: Lawrence Erlbaum Associates.

Bunch, L. (1992). Embracing controversy: Museum exhibitions and the politics of change. *The Public Historian, 14*(3), 64.

Frost, J. (2000). Integrating women and active learning into the US History Survey. *The History Teacher, 33*(3), 363–370.

Gibbons, P. (1998). Non-fiction. In T. Sturm (Ed.), *The Oxford history of New Zealand literature in English*. Auckland: Oxford University Press.

Gregory, F. (1999). *Remembering the nation: Anzac Day and narratives of nationhood*. Unpublished master's thesis, University of Auckland.

Harcourt, M., Fountain G., & Sheehan, M. (2011). Historical significance and sites of memory. *set: Research Information for Teachers, 2*, 26–31.

Jordanova, L. (2000). *History in practice*, London, UK: Arnold.

Kavanagh, G. (1990). *History curatorship*. Washington, DC: Smithsonian Institution Press.

McLean, F. (1998). Museums and the construction of national identity: A review. *International Journal of Heritage Studies, 3*(4), 249.

Mills, H. (1985). *Path to destruction: The origins of the Second World War*. Auckland: Macmillan.

Ministry of Education. (2007). *The New Zealand curriculum*. Wellington: Learning Media.

Ministry of Education. (2009). *Internal assessment resource: Hist/3/2_C5*. Retrieved 10 October 2011 from http://www.tki.org.nz/r/ncea/hist3_2C5_26feb09.pdf

Phillips, J. (1989). War and national identity. In D. Novitz & B. Willmont (Eds.), *Culture and identity in New Zealand* (pp. 91–109). Wellington: GP Books.

Prior, N. (2002). Museums: Leisure between state and distinction. In R. Koshar (Ed.), *Histories of leisure*. Oxford, New York: Berg.

Schlereth, T. (1992). *Cultural history and material culture : everyday life, landscapes, museums*. Charlottesville : University Press of Virginia.

Taylor, T., & Young, C. (2003). *Making history: A guide for the teaching and learning of history in Australian schools*. Melbourne, VIC: Curriculum Corporation.

Worthy, S. (2001). *Communities of remembrance: The memory of the Great War in New Zealand 1915–1939*. Unpublished master's thesis, University of Auckland.

CHAPTER 5

Kua takoto te mānuka: The challenge of contested histories

Paul Enright

Paul Enright is head of the Social Sciences Department at Logan Park High School, Dunedin. He is currently completing his 30th year in the classroom. An enthusiastic educator and grudging administrator, he remains drawn to the challenges and rewards of working with students as they do history. The desire to understand more of what he observes taking place in his classes and apply that understanding in his practice led to an ongoing interest in the pedagogy and methodology of teaching history that has lately extended into active research.

Paul can be contacted at: jjpte@ihug.co.nz

Introduction

Many countries, societies and communities are divided by their common histories. Informed civil discourse, let alone mutual respect and potential reconciliation, depends on recognition of what is contested and why it is contested as steps to understanding. This holds true for many contexts studied—and not studied—in New Zealand secondary history programmes. A new inclusion among the realigned Level 3 standards embeds a "perspectives" strand through NCEA Levels 1, 2 and 3. This strand provides rich opportunities for teachers and students to investigate contested contexts and underlying issues.

This chapter makes the case for taking this a step further and putting investigation of the idea that all history is contested at the heart of redesigned programmes across all NCEA levels. I argue that such an approach makes use of some of the potential unlocked by the New Zealand curriculum and more firmly anchors school history in the essential disciplines of the parent subject that emphasise developing historical thinking among students. I advocate a pragmatic pedagogical approach to shaping the initial programmes, building on many current practices as teachers test and develop strategies to assist student progression through and within the curriculum levels. I also contend that students confident with examining and assessing conflicting historical narratives should be developed through (and beyond) the allocated 3-year span of secondary history.

The approach

Let me state my belief from the outset by paraphrasing William Lamont: controversies in history are its glory, not its weakness (Lamont, 1998). Discussions and debates promoting and defending contesting explanations and analyses, in both class and assignment work, account for some of the best teaching moments and create the most compelling memories, which often emerge in conversation with former students. As I sift through my programmes and strategies while discussing with colleagues how to most effectively implement each level of the realigned history NCEA Achievement Standard, I am increasingly drawn to an approach that puts the contested nature of history at the centre of all inquiry, using this as the engine to drive research, analysis, thinking and comprehension.

The essential element in this approach is provided by the strand that allows exploration of perspectives across all three NCEA levels by adding a Level 3 standard to the revised versions already available at Levels 1 and 2. The new standards offer a path of progression across the three levels. The standard writers made this a central concern during the realignment process, which began in 2008. With only 3 years at the end of secondary education to begin to explore history as a discrete subject, there is an ambitious artificiality in attempting to shoehorn a measured progression from historical novice to competent, independent historian by the time tertiary study beckons, but New Zealand history teachers have traditionally set this as an aim. The new standards in many respects simply give official expression to what is already a community practice.

The relevant strand of the NCEA history matrix currently reads:

Level 1	Level 2	Level 3
AS91004 1.4 Demonstrate understanding of different perspectives of people in an historical event of significance to New Zealanders.	AS91232 2.4 Interpret different perspectives of people in an historical event that is of significance to New Zealanders.	AS 91437 Analyse different perspectives on a contested event of significance to New Zealanders.

At NCEA Level 1, which is Level 6 of the New Zealand curriculum and their first year of studying history as a discrete discipline, students are asked to demonstrate understanding of different perspectives of an historical event. This provides a gentle opportunity to begin exploring critical historical thinking and to challenge naïve assumptions of objective historical truth. The process steps up at Level 2, where the focus is on interpreting different perspectives of people and encourages greater exploration of temporal, spatial, personal and political factors in influencing how events are explained and interpreted. The Level 3 standard develops critical reflection on the nature and purpose of history still further, inviting students to investigate and discuss what Margaret MacMillan (2009) characterises as "the uses and abuses" of history. There are exemplars available, and being developed, and there is planning advice available in the online *History Curriculum Guide*, so rather than duplicate those materials, this discussion focuses on investigating the intent and identifying some underlying pedagogy.

The completed strand is a significant advance. All levels are internally assessed, allowing for a planned independent inquiry whereby history is "taught as both a body and a form of knowledge" (Historical Association, n.d.). Because there are no longer nationally prescribed contexts for study, teachers and students can design local, even individual, programmes. They are free to select contexts for inquiry that ensure engagement and relevance, complementing, supplementing or extending more traditional aspects of their programmes. Aspects of this have been possible ever since internally assessed components were introduced into history, but now significant curriculum time can be invested in the process without any concerns about the potential trade-off against end-of-year examinations. That said, the insights and understanding gained in exploring this set of standards can only deepen the historical skills and historical thinking students bring to bear on all the other standards, both internal and external.

The kind of contexts suited to this standard are those that offer some of the best opportunities to apply the principles, vision and key competencies of *The New Zealand Curriculum* (Ministry of Education, 2007). They also provide opportunities for students to investigate and engage with the past in ways that promote the development of real historical empathy. This kind of empathy, as Foster (2001) argues, moves past imagination, identification and sympathy, using multiple forms of evidence and perspective to develop a deeper appreciation of the chosen context, which leads students to develop "well-grounded but tentative conclusions" that are historically based.

This is particularly the case at Level 3, the only level where the contested history I am advocating is explicitly included. Here the standard, barring further review, requires students to "Analyse different perspectives on a contested event of significance to New Zealanders". Whether couched as an individual inquiry or based on provided sources, tasks measuring the standard will require students to think and write about history in different ways than is currently the norm. They will be encouraged and rewarded for applying approaches and insights drawn from an understanding of disciplinary thinking that require depths of critical knowledge about the context of the contested event and the nature of history that move them beyond the memory-history that presently dominates secondary assessment.

This is a significant change from previous efforts to challenge student notions of historical truth and objectivity by introducing concepts of multiple interpretations and debates over significance, which stretch back to the days of UGC Bursary and Scholarship. Lumped under the unprepossessing category of historiographical knowledge, these were largely approached as teacher-led desultory attempts to map an historical debate through brief extracts (or, worse, summaries) of key analytical statements by leading participants in the debate. These were to be worked into examination essays as "evidence" of additional reading and, optimistically, deeper historical thinking. Anyone venerable enough to have marked the Tudor–Stuart Bursary option will remember the endless critiques of Lawrence Stone's analysis of early modern English families dripping with student disapproval drawn extensively or, more accurately, exclusively from the more considered account of the debate in the most common text of the era. This focus and approach survived the switch from Bursary to Achievement Standards in 2004, where one external standard continued to require discussion of "historical narratives" for the first two years of the new system. When the standards had their first review, the requirement was removed. Not only did this make both essay standards consistent; it also removed a significant barrier to student achievement.

By examining contested histories we help students to identify and critically appraise historical narratives to develop a deeper, more sophisticated understanding of the nature of the discipline. The first steps in developing a 3-year programme to exploit these opportunities involve establishing a clear pedagogical basis, whereby the perspectives standards sit alongside the five other strands, supporting the contexts being studied and contributing to the overall objective: assisting students to develop critical thinking within the disciplinary framework of history. There is room, in our non-prescriptive environment, for pedagogies to evolve in departments in response to and after negotiation with student needs. There is also coherent and challenging pre-existing pedagogical literature to draw on, a selection of which is listed in the readings at the end of this chapter. In the interests of clarity and practicality, I have decided to develop my initial programmes around a core coherent methodology that I can apply immediately and refine as experience, student responses and further research enrich my understanding of processes and issues. Much of the remainder of this chapter focuses on outlining this approach.

Starting the process

There is a challenge that can be given to students at the outset of their formal history education that can make them more receptive to the skills, insights and understanding that come from recognising that history is both contested and constructed. Since reading Hillary Cooper's accounts of teaching history to children in the first years of school (Cooper, 1994, 1995), I have believed that students can comfortably grasp history's second-order concepts to explicitly develop critical thinking at any level if the approach is accessible, participatory and repeated. For the last few years I have used an approach drawn—albeit significantly simplified—from Paul Ricoeur's *Memory, History, and Forgetting* (2004).

Ricoeur identifies memory as the source of history: without memory there can be no history. Various groups, from families through to states and nations, create collective memories, and the set of memories that individuals share with other members of their group help define group identity. These collective memories recover, preserve, reconstruct and transmit past events, creating shared narratives. These narratives are powerful and pre-date and shape individual memory. In this schema, the "operations" of history work to support, correct and sometimes challenge and change collective memory.

Ricoeur's "historical operations" constitute a cycle made of a sequence of phases, distinct but inseparable, along with all the interpretive activities involving decisions about what is to be remembered and what may be forgotten (See Fig 5.1). The bases of these decisions, and the circumstances and conditions that challenge and change these decisions, are at the heart of any investigation of contested history, so this model provides a framework for students to build on.

The first stage of the model is the *documentary phase*. Here, memory is archived as artefacts containing traces of the past, which are collected and preserved. It is also when the first set of decisions and selections about what will be preserved and how it will be recorded are made. The interests of historians, librarians, archivists and others involved in the decisions provide filters for what is remembered and what is forgotten. This collected 'testimony' contain traces of facts, the basis of history. Once collected, it is available for historians to use to identify facts by posing questions: "The documents do not speak unless someone asks them to verify, that is, to make true some hypothesis" (Ricoeur, 2004, p. 177). Here, too, another set of decisions and selections are being made. This second selection in the documentary phase imposes interpretations as some material meets the selected criteria for "history" and other testimony is discarded and "forgotten".

The second stage is explanation/understanding. In this process, historians relate facts to one another to examine their interconnectedness and answer the question 'Why?' through a variety of uses of the connector 'because' (Ricoeur, 2004). In doing so, they move into the third stage, where they produce the historian's representation, turning part of the past into a verbal/textual explanation. The representation is added to the archive of historical materials where it, in turn, will potentially by selected and questioned as the process of historical interpretation continues.

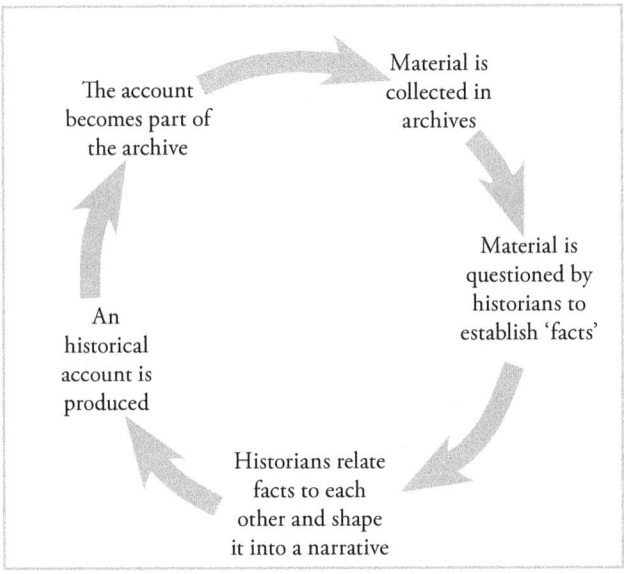

Figure 5.1: Paul Ricoeur's circle of interpretation: A useful focus for discussion

There is an emphasis on the deliberation of these processes that is useful for students to consider and assess, especially if supplemented with equally simplified notions and concepts from Ricoeur's earlier (1990) analysis, *Time and Narrative*. Students are generally quick to see how Ricoeur's description of historical narratives as stories made up of events organised episodically using chronological and temporal criteria challenges the naïve view of an objective, "true" historical record. With extra discussion and analysis of texts, they can also understand that historians, while applying disciplinary rules and criteria, shape events into a story by identifying causes and consequences, assessing change and impact, and applying other concepts and criteria. The insights and disciplinary scepticism they develop from these discussions open their eyes to how and why historical explanations are contested and provide a better understanding of both the sources they consult and the processes they use when they undertake and report on their own research.

I introduced Ricoeur's circle in response to requests from members of a Year 10 social studies class for a working definition of what history is. The requests arose in the course of analysis and discussions we were having about an inquiry into Māori and European interaction prior to Te Tiriti (the Treaty of Waitangi). We had been focusing on investigating the *Boyd* incident and were using the relevant chapter in Peter Woodcock's *The Cultures Collide* (1988). Students were concerned that the primary material provided raised questions they could not answer and that there were clearly missing perspectives. This opened up—for some—questions about how we know what we know and how can we judge what we can trust. Discussing Ricoeur's explanation of the process proved useful and interesting, and I wish I had been quicker to perceive and measure what took place. Some students found the notion of history as something shaped by historians and not something intrinsic to human society exciting and empowering, recognising this gave their own analyses validity if they could support them convincingly. More found the subsequent uncertainty of not being able to draw on a single, agreed analysis initially unnerving. They grasped the essence of the concept, but were disconcerted to varying degrees by the notion. Because the event took place late in the year, I was unable to repeat the process and got limited feedback.

In 2011 I introduced the ideas earlier and explicitly repeated the approach with a subsequent history-focused research study. Repetition over time clearly allowed a greater percentage of the students to assimilate the insights. What caught me out this time was the way students extended the approach to critique source material and accounts in an internet-based study of the contemporary Libyan revolution. This development offered a number of opportunities for discussing issues around reliability and the cross-checking of sources. Again, while the progress made was far from uniform across the cohort, the number of student reviews citing these studies as the most interesting and informative of the course encourage me to believe it is worth persisting with this at Year 10 and building on it in Year 11 history and beyond.

In 2011 I also used Ricoeur's circle with my Year 13 students as they began their year with two research-based internal standards. My impression, drawn from research evaluations and course surveys, is that it provided a challenge to all these relatively inexperienced historians that helped propel them to the next stage of thinking. Discussion and debate on the choice of topic, the nature and quality of sources, and issues of analysis allowed opportunities to encourage metacognitive thinking about the nature of history as both discipline and process. The discussion was usually led by more experienced students. I have noted, informally, the developing insights they often display, and I believe the revised internal Achievement Standards go much further in requiring students to formally record them.

> **My subjective evaluations to date**
>
> Providing students access to such an accessible theoretical overview of history as a process has opened the way to unexpectedly profound insights about the nature of the subject and the role of historians.
>
> Abandoning the comfortable notion of one accepted, verifiable, 'true' historical account may be disconcerting for many students, but for most it is a passing confusion. Many are used to the notions of multiple theories, different proofs and changing explanations from other subjects—and from their own lives.
>
> I can see no aspect of gender, ability or any other differential in how students respond to the challenge of the Ricoeur circle. I suspect the determinant is each individual's intellectual schema and how comfortable they are with the notion of negotiable and mutating 'realities'.

A model of progression

To supplement and extend the direction provided by the Ricoeur circle, I am drawing on an epistemological matrix proposed in a recent work. In *The Challenge of Rethinking History Education* (2011), VanSledright sets out a programme for a "more potent" inquiry-oriented approach to teaching history to replace the dominant approach to the teaching of history in US schools. VanSledright characterises this approach as one that is focused on collective memorisation, transmitted by persistent instruction. He argues that this makes students primarily passive consumers of narratives and results in low cognitive challenge, waning interest and engagement, and even suspicion and resistance, especially from students who find their gender and ethnicity insufficiently or superficially represented in the dominant narrative. Despite the attention given to transmitting knowledge for testing, the National Assessment of Educational Progress given to fourth, eighth and twelfth graders every 4 or 5 years repeatedly suggests that "students do not know very much of the nation's history" or, more precisely, "cannot remember many details of that history that test developers and policy makers think are important to know" (VanSledright, 2011, p. 28).

VanSledright concludes his bleak account of current practices with evidence that the dominant approach is damaging the place and perception of history in schools. He has no doubts what is to blame: "History shorn of its mystery, portrayed as a fait accompli, and whose blemishes are airbrushed to appear as minor irritations loses much of its otherwise riveting appeal" (VanSledright, 2011, p. 28).

The worst aspects of this portrait don't really apply to the situation in New Zealand, even though the underlying sentiments appear from time to time in political and editorial debates (and in NZHTA forums). An approach to national assessment that has emphasised description, explanation and analysis over recall of information, along with prescriptions which, though dated and insufficiently revised, encourage the inclusion of a range of stories and perspectives, have allowed teachers and examiners to work at maintaining the subject's relevance and interest for students.

I believe the most important component for ensuring a brighter picture and better student engagement has been the inclusion of substantial internal assessment components since the 1980s. Internal assessment has allowed teachers and students to explore various modes of presentation as they investigate contexts that range across time and place. History becomes something to do, not just something to learn: mystery, controversy and dispute add lustre and appeal, challenging students to test and weigh explanations and interpretations. The revised Achievement Standards preserve and enhance that capacity. With the perspectives-based strand extended to Level 3 and internally assessed throughout, there are additional opportunities to intrigue and engage students in genuine and meaningful historical debates.

Until the current curriculum began to be incorporated into revised Achievement Standards, implemented from 2011, all history programmes in New Zealand schools drew from a menu of prescribed contexts. To dismiss all those contexts as tried and tired is unfair: the majority fit comfortably into the new curriculum and standards and provide opportunities for examining contested events and interpretations across all levels. The decision to fully exploit the latter potential of the new standards and explore notions of contested history with students places an additional level of importance on decisions made, especially relating to choice of contexts and the relationship between historical narrative and historical disciplines. Students need to be enthused by the possibilities and challenges, but they also need to be reassured that the level of conscious historical thinking and commitment to acquiring historical understanding the approach requires will provide rewards at least commensurate with its demands.

VanSledright provides a model for identifying and measuring student progress in historical thinking and historical understanding that can be used as a broad template for developing aspects of historical thinking and understanding. He identifies three categories of historian—novice, competent and expert—and although he applies these categories across the entire history community, they provide useful categories, competencies and modes of historical thinking to target across the three NCEA levels.

An important qualification

VanSledright doesn't offer his model as a simple, successive pedagogical construct: he is describing stages that stretch from students' first exposure to the discipline through to the experienced academic historian. The translation of VanSledright's novice, competent, expert progression to NCEA levels is my responsibility. It is a flawed and presumptuous application, but it appeals to me as a practising teacher because it provides useful planning targets for building student expertise. When combined with the lack of prescription and an internally assessed outcome, I believe the progression model allows for substantial differentiation and individualisation of instruction as students are monitored.

Progression in historical thinking and historical consciousness is not uniform or linear. A wealth of research shows what teaching experience suggests: each student develops disciplinary skills, insights and the confidence to apply them at different stages (see, for example, Foster & Howson, 2010; Lee, 2004, 2005; Lee & Ashby, 2000). The research also makes it clear that these disciplinary skills and understanding are acquired and refined, not intrinsic. We need to teach them and give students multiple opportunities to apply what they have learnt.

This means there can be no content/skills dichotomy in any sound programme of historical study. Lee and Ashby (2000, p. 200) stress that students still need historical knowledge, but that it must be "understood and grounded" in a developing understanding of history as an academic discipline that is "complex and sophisticated ... with its own procedures and standards".

VanSledright identifies two essential forms of historical understanding typically displayed by novice historians. Initially they are copiers, accepting any historical narrative at face value, making no distinction between the past, in terms of what happened, and history, in terms of what commentators make of what happened. A more sophisticated stage of historical thinking is accessed as the novice becomes a borrower and develops a sense that history is done by cutting and pasting "evidence" together without clear rules or insight into underlying historical concepts that test how and why evidence is selected and configured into an explanatory narrative. It is tempting to see these two student types as

Table 5.1. The Discipline of History

Substantive History "Historical content"		Procedural Ideas of history "Second order Ideas"
What history is about • Substantive concepts like (*franchise, appeasement, dissent*) • Particulars like (*the invasion of the Waikato, Prohibition, nuclear testing in the Pacific*) • Individuals like (*Te Kooti, Elizabeth I, Golda Meir*)	Historians use one to display the other	Ideas about how history is "done" such as • Evidence • Causation • Change • Continuity • Perspectives • Chronology • Historical empathy
This table, based on Lee and Ashby (2000), provides a good discussion point and—if the examples of substantive content are left blank—a resource for either introducing or revising a studied context .		

representing stages on a continuum, and experiential and anecdotal evidence suggests it is fair to assume that most Year 11 students begin their studies in history in one of these camps. The task for history educators is to actively intervene to develop, shape and direct disciplinary thinking and understanding to move students on to the competent and expert levels. The mechanism for doing so lies in developing history domain knowledge by researching contexts that blend substantive and procedural tasks and activities.

In this model of historical learning, students develop from historical *novices* to become *competent* historians when they come to recognise that history results from the selection, organisation and analysis of evidence by investigators using a set of disciplinary rules and procedures to interpret primary and secondary texts. They also recognise that the resulting explanation is presented to others for examination and debate, not as a final 'true' account.

Competent historians become *experts* as they refine and extend their disciplinary knowledge and experience. They understand that history is an academic discipline that seeks to interpret and explain, and that historians 'mine the past', identifying and following seams of evidence, using rule-guided processes and consciously applied criteria to develop historical accounts. They also understand that historical accounts vary and, because they possess tools to analyse and criteria to determine better from less convincing histories, they are comfortable with the notion that different accounts can be sound and legitimate (VanSledright, 2011).

I believe the internally assessed components of the revised Achievement Standards collectively promote the development of expert practice and understanding. The current strands on the history matrix (http://www.tki.org.nz/e/community/ncea/history.php) make this clear:

Level 1	Level 2	Level 3
AS91001 1.1 Carry out an investigation of an historical event, or place, of significance to New Zealanders. **4 credits** Internal	**AS91229** 2.1 Carry out an inquiry of an historical event or place that is of significance to New Zealanders. **4 credits** Internal	**3.1** Carry out research of an historical event, or place, of significance to New Zealanders, using evidence from primary and secondary sources. **5 credits** Internal
AS91002 1.2 Demonstrate understanding of an historical event, or place, of significance to New Zealanders. **4 credits** Internal	**AS91230** 2.2 Examine an historical event, or place, of significance to New Zealanders. **5 credits** Internal	**3.2** Analyse an historical event, or place, to show understanding of its significance to New Zealanders. **5 credits** Internal
AS91004 1.4 Demonstrate understanding of different perspectives of people in an historical event of significance to New Zealanders. **4 credits** Internal	**AS91232** 2.4 Interpret different perspectives of people in an historical event that is of significance to New Zealanders. **5 credits** Internal	**3.4** Analyse different perspectives on a contested event of significance to New Zealanders. **5 credits** Internal

The process and product standards (the first two strands) provide opportunities for students to do 'real' history and develop an understanding of how to find, select, weigh and structure evidence. Although it is hard to tell just from the standard titles, each level seeks to build on what students have previously achieved, aiming for an approach similar to VanSledright's expert by Level 3. The perspectives strand pushes this objective more directly, moving students from the recognition that people can have different understandings of and responses to historical events, through to requiring them to critically examine and even evaluate the relative validity of perspectives on an event that is the focus of contending interpretations.

I have believed from the time internal assessment was included in history programmes that the insights, experience and increased confidence in applying historical skills developed in these tasks and assignments provide the subject's most lasting legacy for its students. I also believe that progress in this area informs and refines progress in external assessments. As we become increasingly able to reinforce links between the two approaches to measuring historical learning, and use the new control over the level of content information to allow greater focus on developing understanding in depth among all students, these connections can only increase.

My department has made slow and measured changes to teaching programmes as we have waited for the dust of standards reviews and revisions to settle. As the Level 3 standards have coalesced, it has become easier to develop some medium-term plans to begin to exploit new opportunities and approaches. In broad terms, we are looking to move students on from a targeted but gentle introduction in Year 11, which draws on family-based research for two of the internals and provides opportunities to discuss and apply the Ricoeur circle using popular, engaging contexts. The Year 12 course will extend the analysis and sharpen the focus with directed, New Zealand-based research and contexts that develop insights into concepts such as revolution and dissent, with some comparative studies. Over those two levels we will develop an understanding of history as a discipline alongside the students' content-based studies. At Year 13, however, fostering historical thinking and historical comprehension will be at the centre of the history programme from 2013. By this stage students deserve the challenges and insights this approach offers. Such an approach will prepare them well for the short-term objectives of Year 13 assessment while equipping them with bigger, deeper and more lasting insights.

Among the options being considered, the frontrunner is one that requires a substantial reorganisation of the current programme. It would see students start the year with a common task on a contested issue or event in a taught context. This allows teaching and discussion around essential understandings and procedures regarding evidence, perspective, purpose, and so on. We operate a (largely) open-entry policy to Year 13 history, so an initial task like this will also allow some extra individual attention to ensure new historians are effectively inducted. An individual research project on an area of contested history chosen by the student in consultation with the class teacher and other advisers will follow.

After presentations and formal debrief, we will proceed to a formal study of a conventional context. This will be a more demanding context than in Year 12; currently we are looking at the development of English colonialism, using case studies to examine its development from Ireland in the late 16th century to New Zealand in the 19th and 20th centuries. As we study the chosen context(s), we will explicitly incorporate the procedural skills, disciplines and understandings developed in the first two terms' activities to enhance students' analytical and evaluative understanding.

The objective of this approach is to develop students as independent historical thinkers. On the mundane level of professional accountability, this aim is consistent with the bolder aspects of the vision of *The New Zealand Curriculum* (Ministry of Education, 2007). It seems to be consistent with the message that has been sent by 5 years of responses to student surveys across all three levels we offer: students find inquiry and research in history to be both the most challenging and the most satisfying elements in their courses. They want more time, especially for discussion, sharing progress, problems and solutions, and, most clearly, some sort of plenary forum where they can see and hear what others have done. We can do this by practising what we preach and judiciously selecting content (not abandoning it as some seem to fear) to allow time to consider, reflect, evaluate and apply the learning that results.

What might this look like?

I am naturally wary of tables and diagrams that imply or even impose an order or sequence that is highly debatable. This is especially the case with learning and progression in history, where my experience and my reading point to developments being individual and eccentric. That said, I do believe my intended approach demonstrates a broad process (see Figure 5.2).

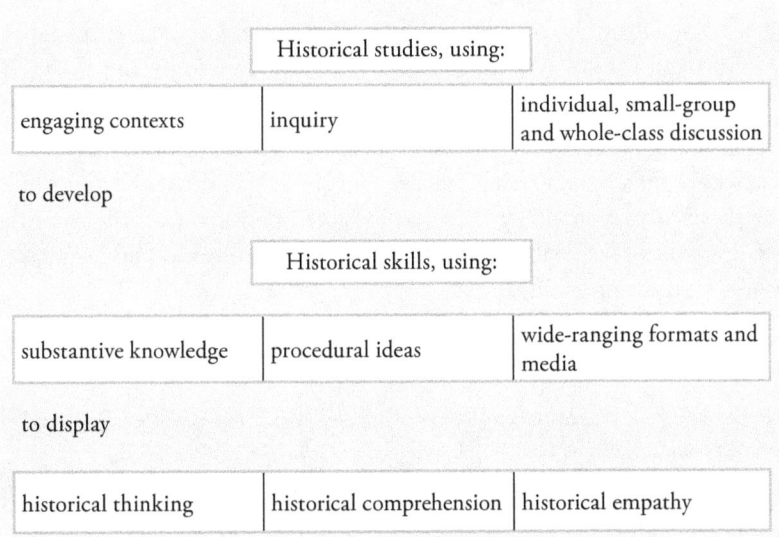

Figure 5.2. An Historical Process

The next steps?

An approach that sets off in a significantly different direction must be reviewed and adjusted. Formal and informal surveying of student responses together with critical appraisal of documentation and delivery by colleagues within and beyond the department are essential. I am also hopeful that we will develop and extend the fledgling research community developing within our school and our local history community. To this end there are at least three clear lines of research to pursue:

- a longitudinal study similar to the work undertaken by Peter Lee, Rosalyn Ashby and others, investigating the development of student historical thinking and historical consciousness, and the nature and evidence of progression as the students work through the perspectives strand of the standards
- a longitudinal study investigating student pick-up of the ideas in Ricoeur's circle to see if there are any ongoing effects on approaches to research, evidence and interpretation
- a follow-up study to gather evidence of the practical value of historical skills and thinking as students move into tertiary study and the wider world.

Undertaking a selection of these lines of research poses significant challenges for any practising teacher, but it is fitting that they also offer the possibility of providing data and insights to inform discussions on the contribution of internal assessment to student learning—a hotly contested aspect of history teaching.

References

Cooper, H. (1994). *The teaching of history in primary schools: Implementing the Revised National Curriculum* (2nd ed.). London, UK: David Fulton Publishers.

Cooper, H. (1995). *History in the early years: Teaching and learning in the first three years of school*. London, UK: Routledge.

Foster, S. J. (2001). Historical empathy in theory and practice. In O.L. Davis Jr., E. A. Yeager, & S. J. Foster (Eds.), *Historical empathy and perspective taking in the social sciences* (pp. 167–181). London, UK: Rowman & Littlefield Publishers.

Foster, S., & Howson, J. (2010). School history students' 'big picture' of the past. *International Journal of Historical Learning, Teaching and Research*, 9(2). Retrieved 12 September 2011 from http://www.history.org.uk/resources/secondary_resource_4014_149.html

Historical Association. *TEACH: Teaching emotive and controversial history, 3–19*. Retrieved 31 October 2009 from http://www.history.org.uk/resources/secondary_resource_780.html

Lamont, W. (Ed.). (1998). *Historical controversies and historians*. London and New York: Routledge.

Lee, P. (2004). "Walking backwards into tomorrow": Historical consciousness and understanding history. *International Journal of Historical Learning, Teaching and Research*, 4(1). Retrieved 12 September 2011 from http://www.history.org.uk/resources/secondary_resource_4857_149.html

Lee, P. (2005). Historical literacy: Theory and research. *International Journal of Historical Learning, Teaching and Research*, 5(1). Retrieved 12 September 2011 from http://www.history.org.uk/resources/secondary_resource_4859_149.html

Lee, P., & Ashby, R. (2000). Progression in historical understanding among students ages 7–14. In P. N. Stearns, P. Seixas, & S. Wineburg. *Knowing, teaching and learning history: National and international perspectives*. New York, NY: New York University Press.

MacMillan, M. (2009). *The uses and abuses of history*. London, UK: Profile Books.

Ministry of Education. (2007). *The New Zealand curriculum*. Learning Media: Wellington.

Ricoeur, P. (1990). *Time and narrative*, vol. 1, trans. K. McLachlin & D. Pellauer. Chicago, IL: University of Chicago Press.

Ricoeur, P. (2004). *Memory, history and forgetting*, trans. K. Blamey & D. Pellauer. Chicago, IL: University of Chicago Press.

VanSledright, B. A. (2011). *The challenge of rethinking history education: On practices, theories and policy*. New York, NY: Routledge (Taylor & Francis).

Woodcock, P. (1988). *The cultures collide: The contact period of New Zealand history, 1769–1840*. Auckland: Macmillan.

Further reading

Online sources

Ministry of Education. 2010. *New Zealand curriculum guides: Senior secondary: History*. Retrieved 25 August 2011 from http://seniorsecondary.tki.org.nz/Social-sciences/History.

New Zealand history online: http://www.nzhistory.net.nz/

Davison, M. *Teaching and learning history*. Retrieved 3 July 2012 from http://www.nzhistory.net.nz/classroom/teaching-and-learning-history

Davison, M. *Teaching emotive and controversial history*. Retrieved 3 July 2012 from http://www.nzhistory.net.nz/classroom/teaching-emotive-and-controversial-history

Sheehan, M. *It ain't necessarily so: The role of school history in a meaningful education*. Retrieved 25 August 2008 from http://www.nzhistory.net.nz/classroom/the-classroom/teachers-toolbox/the-role-of-school-history

Documents

Cole, E. A. (Ed.). (2007). *Teaching the violent past: History education and reconciliation*. New York, NY: Rowman and Littlefield.

Dauenhauer, B., & Pellauer, D. Paul Ricoeur. In E. N. Zalta (Ed.), *The Stanford Encyclopedia of Philosophy* (Summer 2011 Edition). Retrieved from http://plato.stanford.edu/archives/sum2011/entries/ricoeur. [This is a very accessible introduction to Ricoeur and his work.]

Hodgkin, K., & Radstone, S. (Eds.). (2009). *Memory, history, nation: Contested pasts*. New Brunswick, NJ: Transaction Publishers.

Rusen, J. (2006). Historical consciousness: Narrative structure, moral function and ontogenetic development. In P. Seixas (Ed.), *Theorizing historical consciousness*. Toronto, ON: University of Toronto Press.

Seixas, P. (2000). 'Schweigen! Die kinder!' Or, does postmodern history have a place in schools. In P. N. Stearns, P. Seixas, & S. Wineburg (Eds.), *Knowing, teaching and learning history: National and international perspectives*. New York, NY: New York University Press.

Stearns, P. N., Seixas P., & Wineburg S. (2000). *Knowing, teaching and learning history: National and international perspectives*. New York, NY: New York University Press.

CHAPTER 6

Learning to think historically: Developing historical thinking through internally assessed research projects

MARK SHEEHAN AND JONATHAN HOWSON

Dr Mark Sheehan is a senior lecturer at Victoria University Faculty of Education, where he teaches courses in secondary school history and curriculum theory. He has been involved in history education for over 25 years as a writer, researcher and educator, and his current research focuses on the development of disciplinary thinking in history as well as the place of knowledge in the New Zealand curriculum.

Mark can be contacted at: Mark.sheehan@vuw.ac.nz

Jonathan Howson has been a secondary history and politics teacher working at inner city comprehensives in London. In 2005 he left to join the Institute of Education, University of London, as an academic researcher and lecturer of history in education. The research projects he has been involved with and his publications include work on historical consciousness, the aims and purposes of history education, identity, and teaching about the Holocaust in England. His last position before moving to New Zealand in 2011 was deputy head of the Academic Department for Humanities at IOE and he is currently a researcher on a Teaching and Learning Research Initiative (TLRI) project that is investigating how history students learn to think historically.

Jonathan can be contacted at: jonohowson@hotmail.com

MARK SHEEHAN and JONATHAN HOWSON

Introduction

How do history students learn to think historically and, in particular, to understand how the discipline of history operates? Novices typically develop expertise in a disciplinary field by emulating what experts in the field actually do. For example archaeology students work with archaeologists on excavations and botany students conduct experiments with botanists on plants. The extent to which students develop historical thinking when they conduct internally assessed research studies is the focus of this chapter. It is argued that history students at secondary school are being inducted into the discipline of history and as novices they are more likely to develop disciplinary competence and expertise in historical thinking by conducting historical research, because this is what historians (as experts in the field) actually do. Developing disciplinary competence and expertise in a particular field is essential for academic success in the 'knowledge age' as it is through disciplinary thinking that students 'learn to do things with knowledge, to use knowledge in inventive ways, in new contexts and combinations … [and] to enter and navigate the constantly shifting networks and flows of knowledge that are a feature of 21st century life' (Bolstad & Gilbert, 2012: 32). It is also through disciplinary thinking that students (as novices) shift from focusing on the superficial features of knowledge to develop the characteristics of experts who tend to 'think in terms of deep structures or the underlying principles of knowledge' (Bolstad & Gilbert, 2012: 15). This chapter draws on the early analysis of a Teaching and Learning Research Initiative (TLRI) study that is examining how history students learn how to think historically through standards-based internally assessed research projects. Initial findings indicate that not only do students who engage in this style of learning demonstrate high levels of intrinsic motivation, but also by engaging with the processes of how historical knowledge is produced when they conduct research, they develop a sophisticated understanding of the interpretative and contested features of the discipline.

The context

Establishing the intellectual credibility of internal assessment at this point in time is important because this component of the NCEA qualification continues to garner criticism from some quarters that it is demotivating and lacks academic credibility. For example, one of New Zealand's most prestigious state secondary boys' schools recently largely eliminated the internal assessment component of NCEA at Year 11. The principal claimed that this was because the "learning style and nature of most boys suited external exams", there had been a "decline in motivation and the work ethic of students", and internal assessment undermined "the coherence of individual subjects" (Morris, 2010). The principal's stance on internal assessment is not out of step with the view among a number of high-decile schools that internal assessment lacks academic credibility and that external examinations are a more valid measure of students' intellectual development. The media are also typically critical of internal assessment. For example, a recent article in *North and South* attacked the integrity of NCEA internal assessment by alleging that the government body responsible for examinations (the New Zealand Qualifications Authority) "fudged the figures" to make it appear that moderators and teachers agreed on the internal assessment mark for students' work (Coddington, 2011). The article was deemed "unfair and unbalanced" by the authority that monitors journalistic standards (New Zealand Press Council, 2012), yet it was stoutly defended in subsequent editions by the editor and commentators.

These criticisms tap into ongoing public concerns over how effectively internal assessment is preparing young people for the 21st century in an age of growing youth unemployment, increasing academic requirements to access tertiary courses, and commentators who argue that the endless diet of YouTube, wikis, twitters and blogs that are so prevalent in adolescents' social lives is influencing young people's thinking patterns. The latter argument is popularly known as the "Is Google making us stupid?" thesis, as epitomised in Nicholas Carr's *Atlantic* article of the same name (Carr, 2008), which implies that young people in the 21st century can no longer concentrate for any length of time on complex tasks. In light of these concerns and the high-stakes nature of secondary school assessment at this level, this 2-year TLRI study is examining the extent to which internally assessed research projects motivate secondary school history students to develop disciplinary competence and expertise (or what is known as historical thinking). The researchers adopted a mixed method qualitative approach to gathering the data (Levstik & Barton, 2008), including interviewing, focus groups and documentary analysis. The focus of the analysis has been on how students engage with the particular methodologies, vocabulary and concepts of history, as well as the contested and interpretive nature of how knowledge is produced in the discipline. This chapter draws on the first year of the project (2011), in which data was gathered from 42 senior history students in three New Zealand schools (two in the South Island and one in the North). In the second year of the study, two other schools have joined the project (one in Auckland and one in Wellington) and the total number of student participants in the project is expected to be 80–85. The study has also been expanded to examine the role of teachers in the research process (including how they make decisions when they are marking internal assessment assignments).

Thinking historically

The shape of inquiry-based research projects in New Zealand has drawn heavily on proponents of the disciplinary approach to history education (Lee & Ashby 2000; Seixas 1997, 1994; Shemilt 1987), whose aim has been to teach about the nature and status of historical knowledge and rational constructions of the past that are informed by a developing concept of evidence. To achieve academic success at this level, students are also required to engage in a form of 'critical literacy', in which they draw on disciplinary knowledge and understanding to make sense of what they study (Mcdonald & Thornley, 2009, p. 56). In history, students need to be able to read and understand large amounts of text, and to develop a grasp of specialised vocabulary and discipline-based methodologies (Sturtevant & Linek, 2004). They must become familiar with aspects of the concepts and principles of the domain of the academic discipline as negotiated by experts in the field and this "cannot be acquired purely from everyday experiences" but rather requires "systematic instruction" (Alexander,

1997). Lee (2004) argues that although history may be diverse, it has some characteristic organising ideas and these can be divided into substantive concepts that are linked to content (the substance of history) and what he calls the "meta-historical" or second-order concepts that are central to the framework of the discipline (such as change, continuity and significance). Understanding how these second-order concepts operate in history are largely counterintuitive (Wineburg, 2001) but they are important in shaping student's ideas about the nature and status of historical accounts, what counts as evidence in history and the interpretive features of the discipline.

Motivation

The study identified a number of key factors that motivate history students to engage successfully with disciplinary knowledge in history through research projects and demonstrated that many of these students are learning something of the critical, disciplinary tools that historians use, including the ability to evaluate competing versions of the past. With regard to epistemic cognition, there was evidence that students use a range of ideas, tools and strategies, some more sophisticated than others, and that these students are engaging with these questions at a deep conceptual level. In this type of learning, especially with regard to second-order concepts, the high level of motivation among students appears to be the result of the personal interest students had in their particular topic choices (they typically had considerable autonomy over what they study). This indicates that what is motivating students may be more than simply the extrinsic motivation of gaining assessment credits (Meyer et al., 2009) as participants in this study appeared to be intrinsically motivated to develop sophisticated levels of disciplinary expertise as part of structured learning through research projects. This is especially apparent in regards to their understanding of the contested and interpretive features of the subject and may be explained by students engaging with the processes of how knowledge is produced in the discipline, including how historians make and critique truth claims.

Themes

Part of the interview process included an attempt to understand what kinds of ideas about history the participants were working with. The semi-structured interview format, with its focus questions, prompts and follow-on questions, allowed researchers to better understand how students think about the past. The questions employed to do this were variations of the following:

- Why are there different versions and interpretations of the past?
- Why do you think there are different ways of accounting for the past?
- Are there better ways of thinking about or approaching the past than others?

At this stage findings have been organised under a number of thematic headings articulated by the participants, such as ideas concerning bias in history, and a range of ideas within this particular theme. The reporting at this stage concerns what students are saying on the themes they have identified in response to researchers' broad questions on the nature of historical knowledge. Analysis is a complex matter because the range of ideas about particular themes is not uniform (some ideas are of a higher order than others), they overlap, and sometimes are contradictory. For example, a number of students considered the detection of bias in historical sources to be an important objective of history education. Others argued that this is not necessarily the case because all sources from the past are biased in the sense that they are products of their time and were not created for the particular purpose of reconstructing the past. This also led to some interesting distinctions being made between bias and ideas on perspective taking, some of which will be discussed below.

Most discussions about aspects of history tended to encompass multiple second-order concepts in addition to substantive concepts and content. For example, a lesson on the ratification process of the Treaty of Waitangi might include a discussion on perspective taking in history, the significance of events in creating accounts of the past, ideas about change over time, and the evidence on which these historical accounts were/are created. The key research themes identified from the data gathering included:

- perspective and bias in history
- concerns over a balanced view of the past
- the reliability or utility of sources
- ideas about historical truth and the role of facts
- critical approaches to history
- the nature of historical accounts
- controversial issues in history
- the effect of time and distance from past events and how we engage with them
- ideas on objectivity
- ideas about learning lessons from the past.

Bias and perspective

When asked why it is that we have different interpretations of the past, much of the discussion revolved around ideas on perspective and bias put forward by the participants. Peter argued that "all sources are biased because that's just how it is and I don't believe you can be completely impartial about something, because you just can't". He reasoned that this bias is not necessarily malicious but that we have different interpretations of the past:

> because it is really human nature, it's a part of everyone's personality and everyone has their own different set of values and morals. I may value different things to what people sitting in this room value, and so events that happen may have bigger impacts on me as opposed to everyone else, where events that happened to them may have a bigger impact on them depending on what they value.

Many of the participants had similar views to Peter: objectivity and truth are not really attainable in history, partly because human beings attach significance to events in the past in different ways, and the explanatory account that incorporates these events will thus take different forms. John expressed this idea elegantly:

> I would put facts down as the bones perhaps, the building blocks and I would put interpretation as the colours if that makes more sense. It's how you see things and what significance you attach to different things. You can show 20 people a film and they can all tell you the plot of the film

and then pick up on different things. So there are the facts of the film and there is what people take away from it.

Some of these students were clearly able to grasp the interpretive nature of the discipline and were able to move beyond bias or perspectives informed by previous experience. There was also evidence that some students were able to tap into a more complex understanding associated with the nature and status of historical knowledge and what counts as evidence for claims made about the past. For example, Luke at first argued that truth is attainable when accounting for the past where there is, say, video evidence to support a particular claim. The researcher asked him if this was possible if the history sought to account for individual or collective rationales for action—to explain an aspect of the past that was about reasons for doing things. Luke conceded that this would not be possible:

> It's something you will never truly know. You can guess at it, but you can never be completely certain. The person might lie or have changed their mind over time so you can never actually know what the person is thinking. For example, I might have eaten cake and thought it was average, then a week later I thought the cake was much tastier than I did before. And now in my opinion if you asked me what I thought the cake tasted like I would say it tasted really, really good even though I didn't before, but now I decided it did.

In this case the future can change what we say about the past without making one account more valid than the other. The two accounts of cake eating are valid for their time, although different.

A number of students understood that while two accounts of the past covering the same events (but based on different questions) are likely to produce different accounts, both are valid as long as they are based on the protocols of disciplinary thinking. Mary pointed out that although perspectives are important, the accounts that are generated from them are dependent on the questions we ask. She claims:

> there's facts and then there's, well, it depends on your questions a lot as well, and it's talking about people's views towards something. What you are looking for is not a truthful account or something, but the way that people differed or were the same in their views.

Some participants had arranged notions of bias into their own categories, such as this from Max:

> My thoughts would be to do with different forms of bias such as ... a national bias, created during wars or when you are trying to antagonise another country, and there is another form of bias which you get when you have certain elections; you have an identity bias, which is when you associate certain things with certain political leaders. That's when you get people segregating because their opinions start differentiating because of their views on that certain political leader, even though perhaps their views may be incorrect. There is also mob mentality you get when you conform to ideals of the greater, because you want to fit in. I just think who people are and what we interpret history as, that's the reason we have different interpretations, because everybody is different.

Not all students, however, had a sophisticated grasp of the second order concepts of the discipline and some were working with a weaker notion that bias was a consequence of there being less in the way of modern freedoms. For example Tessa claimed:

> In a way, back a long time ago, then it was the leader wrote the history or told people to write the history for them, but now it's like diverse. People write books and they're more free.

Such notions, however, were unusual in this cohort. More typically Catherine expressed a more subtle understanding of the nature of change and continuity over time. She was aware that she needed to be on guard over issues such as propaganda, and that this may be at least as difficult for those in the present as it was for past actors:

> the presence of skewed information is always present, especially when dishing out information is so easy these days ... [but] I think that as long as you keep your beliefs and are aware that there is propaganda out there, I think you can maintain a sense of self and not be misguided so easily.

In a similar vein Belinda describes her experience in the context of her reflections on the interpretive nature of history:

> Well, we are looking at a lot of people's accounts of it so if our work is completely biased towards the way they thought, so, in my project a lot of my sources are people that came after the time, so it's their perspectives of what it was like, but they weren't involved and so this inevitably biases my work because of the sources I find, as well as the fact that the moment you choose whether you're for or against a subject when you are going to write about it that instantly makes a bias anyway.

Conclusion

What is clear from the data is that the participants have expressed a range of ideas about both the substantive and the second order aspects of history, which demonstrates that many are developing a sophisticated grasp of the disciplinary features of the subject. Engaging with internally assessed research projects is also offering them a chance to address their preconceptions, develop critical thinking skills and address complex conceptual matters directly associated within the discipline of history. Furthermore while these students are certainly extrinsically motivated to achieve high grades in internally assessed projects, they are also intrinsically motivated to go well beyond what is required of them to achieve academic success and grapple with the interpretive and contested features of the disciplinary knowledge.

Afterword

An early version of this chapter ('Developing historical thinking through research projects: A New Zealand case study') was jointly presented by the authors at the New Zealand Association for Research in Education Conference at Bay of Plenty Polytechnic (1 December 2011), and a full paper was presented by Mark Sheehan (with TLRI teacher/researchers Paul Enright and Lara Hearn-Rollo) at the American Educational Research Association in Vancouver, 15 April 2012). All names of students have been changed. For further information on this project and subsequent publications/presentations please contact the authors and/or see: www.tlri.org.nz

References

Alexander, P. A. (1997). Mapping the multidimensional nature of domain learning: The interplay of cognitive, motivational and strategic forces. *Advances in Motivation and Achievement, 10*, 213–250.

Bolstad, R. & Gilbert, J. (2012). *Supporting future oriented learning and teaching: A New Zealand perspective.* Wellington: Ministry of Education.

Carr, N. (2008). Is Google making us stupid?: What the internet is doing to our brains. *Atlantic*, July/August. Retrieved from http://www.theatlantic.com/magazine/archive/2008/07/is-google-making-us-stupid/306868/

Coddington, D. (2011). Blowing the whistle. *North & South, 304*, 50-56.

Editorial. (2012, March). *New Zealand Listener*, 24-30.

Goodson, I. (1983). *School subjects and curriculum change*. London, UK: Falmer.

Lee, P. (2004). Understanding history. In P. Seixas (Ed.), *Theorizing historical consciousness* (pp. 129-164). Toronto, ON: University of Toronto Press.

Lee, P., & Ashby, R. (2000). Progression in historical understanding among students ages 7-14. In P. Stearns, P. Seixas, & S. Wineburg (Eds.), *Knowing, Teaching and learning history* (pp. 199-222). New York, NY: New York University Press.

Levstik, L., & Barton, K. (Eds.). *Researching history education: Theory, method and context*. New York, NY: Routledge.

Mcdonald, T., & Thornley, C. (2009). Critical literacy for academic success in secondary school: Examining students' use of disciplinary knowledge. *Critical Literacy: Theories and Practices, 3*(2), 56-68.

Meyer, L. H., McClure, J., Walkey, F., Weir K. F., & McKenzie, L. (2009). Secondary student motivation orientations and standards-based achievement outcomes. *British Journal of Educational Psychology, 79*, 273-293.

Morris, J. (2010). *Extension of IGCSE to Form 5 in 2011*. Auckland Grammar School. Retrieved 26 April 2010 from http://www.ags.school.nz/content/academic/extension_of_igcse_to_form_5_in_2011.html

New Zealand Press Council. (2012). *Case Number: 2213 PPTA against North & South*. Retrieved from http://www.presscouncil.org.nz/display_ruling.php?case_number=2213Cached

Seixas, P. (1994). Students' understanding of historical significance. *Theory and Research in Social Education, 22*, 281-304.

Seixas, P. (1997). Mapping the terrain of historical significance. *Social Education, 61*(1), 22-27.

Shemilt, D. (1987). Adolescent ideas about evidence and methodology in history. In C. Portland (Ed.), *The history curriculum for teachers* (pp. 39-61). London, UK: Heinemann.

Sturtevant, E. G., & Linek, W. M. (2004). *Content literacy: An inquiry-based case approach*. Upper Saddle River, NJ: Pearson Education.

Wineburg, S. (2001). *Historical thinking and other unnatural acts: Charting the future of teaching the past*. Philadelphia, PA: Temple University Press.

"… to subscribe to populist and mythic constructions of the past is to remain trapped in the codes and culture of the street gang, to invoke persuasive and partial histories that reinforce simple truths and even simpler hatreds."

Denis Shemilt[1]

---

1 D. Shemilt. (2000). The caliph's coin: The currency of narrative frameworks in history. In P. Stearns, P. Seixas, & S. Wineburg (Eds.), *Knowing, teaching and learning history: National and international perspectives* (pp. 83–101). New York, NY: New York University Press.

CHAPTER 7

Facebook and teaching history

LARA HEARN-ROLLO

Lara Hearn-Rollo is currently on secondment to the University of Otago, College of Education from her position as the Learning Area Leader of the Humanities Department at Queen's High School in Dunedin. She has been teaching for nearly 20 years across a range of schools of varying decile. Since returning home to Dunedin in 2008 she has become increasingly involved in the Otago history community, which has culminated in her becoming chair of the new national executive of NZHTA. Lara has also been actively involved in the writing of the aligned standards at Levels 1, 2 and 3, and of the Teaching and Learning Guide, and has run several professional development courses for history teachers in the South Island.

Lara can be contacted at: lara.hearn-rollo@otago.ac.nz

Introduction

What is teaching if it is not a form of social networking? For that matter, what is education if it is not social networking? Yet many still have this idea that tools such as Facebook, Ning and MySpace are to be discouraged or avoided in schools. The biggest concern, it seems, is the opportunity for undesirable behaviour to occur on blogs, Facebook pages and online communities anonymously. There have been a number of issues that have seen Facebook make the news, from lack of privacy to personal details being used inappropriately, to cyber-bullying. There have been well-publicised stories of teachers compromised and even dismissed for unwisely or improperly using social media in their personal and professional lives.

However, as with everything, there are positives and negatives to Facebook and I believe the key to using this platform for educational purposes is to view all the associated interactions as occurring in a learning environment. This allows you and your students to access an increasing number of history-focused educational pages on Facebook from college lecturers, history organisations, and institutions with a historical focus (such as national archives and school history departments) from around the world. It is, I suspect, increasingly being seen as a vehicle to distribute information and advice which is not readily accessible in the classroom.

My own experience using Facebook in a teaching environment developed from what appeared to me to be students' innate curiosity about their teachers. This was particularly obvious to me as a new teacher in my current school, with no previous history with the students in front of me. The issues of who is this person, where does she come from, does she really think she can teach us, etc. led to them trying to find out more about me, and many of them turned to Facebook, the platform they knew and used to keep in touch with their friends. Many of them, finding that my personal page was private and they couldn't access it, asked to be my "friend", which in itself opened up a number of issues and concerns I didn't want to experience first-hand.

One day when I was pondering these issues and listening to my Year 12s, it struck me that Facebook offers something that traditional platforms such as Moodle don't: it is already part of my students' lives and 'an environment of choice'. The more I thought about it, the more it seemed that Facebook had a place in teaching. My students had quick access to each other through Facebook Chat, they could upload links to photos and sites of interest to them, put up notes, essays and booklists, hold discussions and set up events, and they could also start analysing and discussing documents they came across in their research. They were already using it, so the only person needing to upskill was me!

Because it is a central element in students' communication network, it also offers an ideal means of communication should school be closed for whatever reason—usually snow days in Dunedin. I would still be able to contact my girls and let them know there was work up on Moodle, or that they needed to do some additional reading and where that could be found. As one of my students, Meghan, explains:

> with students these days becoming more digitally aware it seemed only natural that we would be using a Facebook page as a means to connect with our history teacher and classmate at any time, whether in school or out of school.

It seemed that Facebook could prove to be invaluable outside the classroom.

It was out of these musings, and the ongoing need to decline more students as 'friends' on my personal Facebook page, that the *History at Queen's* page was developed. After looking at the different options for pages and groups, I decided to set up a page that was linked to my existing account. This meant that students had to 'like' the page, and it meant that anything I put up automatically went on their news feed, or wall, where they could comment on it. Sitting as it did on this feed meant that links and additional comments were all displayed, easily accessible and able to be viewed immediately. The impact of this news feed was further enhanced when students signed up to mobile notifications. These notifications via text instantly appealed to some students because it meant they were never out of touch with what was happening—and students are never very far from their mobiles, so it was another means of instant communication.

As responses began to accumulate on my wall the educational potential emerged in new and exciting ways that rapidly moved my sense of how Facebook could be used—far beyond notions of it being an easy and popular means of communicating information. Elaine Childs (2008) argues in *Using Facebook as a Teaching Tool* that "the most successful aspect of the page was the wall as students posted informal comments and questions there". The wall provides a place where you and your students can place links to other sites, documents, YouTube clips, media items, etc. The comment and share facilities mean that discussion can occur online about the content and concepts within the documents or links, and questions can be raised as students think of them.

The news feed, or wall, therefore provides not only the ability for me and my students to 'talk', but also, as Childs (2008) notes, it is a forum for "informal, horizontal exchange". This type of exchange has happened increasingly frequently, and in her evaluation of the use of Facebook in learning, one student, Emma, noted that

> the whole class was also able to have multiple conversations online, and because we could see the questions or comments others posted it helped us answer or figure out what we needed to know. Facebook allowed not only Ms Hearn to help us but to also help each other with schoolwork and learning.

Not all friends on the page are current students. Also watching the page are past students (who often give advice), other history teachers, and people with an interest in history. In short, a small new learning community has developed, which is geared towards providing advice, guidance and additional resources for my students. Their learning, and their ability to access other historians and history students, has been further enhanced with the development of other history pages, such as *Year 13 History at Logan Park* and *Year 13 History Wellington College*. Recently there have been others set up in Canterbury, with Christchurch Girls' and Villa Maria now online and providing a place for the girls to check for ideas. Linking with these sites means that my girls have access to a wealth of expertise and experience that was previously unheard of, and it has allowed my students to access some of the main benefits of Facebook, as outlined by Towner, Van Horn and Parker (2007):

> networking and social communication capabilities can greatly enhance the learning experience of both the teacher and the student. [This occurs because of the ability to tap] ... into a greater number of learning styles, providing relief from the traditional lecture format, and by building [on] top of the community already established by the students themselves. (p. 13)

How do I use Facebook as a teaching tool?

It is a method of communication, a growing network that expands students' thinking and horizons, connecting me to them, them to me, them to each other, them and other history students around the country, and them to other subject experts. I use it to:

- post links to sites of interest

- post about significant historical events, such as Anzac Day or Parihaka, and give them links to encourage further exploration of these topics
- upload essays and other exemplars and notes on internal assessment
- remind them of upcoming deadlines
- alert them to events, or let them know when I am in school over the holidays.

Students also understand what it provides. For Emma, Facebook was a learning tool:

> [If I] needed to ask a question when working at home I could just post a comment or question on this page and get pretty much an instant response. This was very useful as it meant I could get my work or study done efficiently and with help if I needed it. It was also good because Ms Hearn could post useful links or reminders to us over Facebook.

Couillard claims that "Facebook has the potential to become a learning network with structure and flexibility" (2010, p. 5). This is what quickly became the purpose of the Queen's page and what I believe has been achieved. It turned out that it can be used as a very effective tool to support independent learning and encourage students to share experiences and discoveries while supporting each other. Lauren describes it like this:

> Facebook as a learning tool allows students and teachers to share external links to online resources and also allows all to post questions about their subject, both students and teachers can answer these questions allowing discussions. While doing homework or research on the computer, a lot of us do have Facebook open in tabs as well, this allowed us to see any new posts or comments relating to our learning instantly.

This idea of linking to external sources and holding conversations is echoed in Ayer's work, where he claims that the best thing computers have done for history is to facilitate the "deepening and broadening of professional conversation". He notes that the potential was recognised from the very beginning: "early in the internet's development, in the days before the Web, historians used discussion lists on the internet to post questions, offer interpretations, and solicit advice" (Ayers, 1999).

Students' use of Facebook is intuitive and pragmatic. They use it to ask questions; check out things like instructions, deadlines and potential sources or avenues of interest; comment on others' questions and help answer them; and (occasionally) remind me of things. They will also post links to something they have read or seen that interests them. It has become a living document for my students—full of advice, resources and additional information—which, if they wish, they can trawl back through to the start to find any other interesting comments. As Ayers notes, "students read course materials at all times of the day, talk with one another and collaborate, and embark on research projects that would have been impossible just a few years ago" (Ayers, 1999). Students are therefore connected to their learning when they want to be and in their own time, and not just between the hours of 9.00am and 3.30pm. It is not unusual to have questions come through on the page late at night—usually after most non-adolescent people have gone to bed.

The Facebook page became the first port of call for students when working on their internal assessments. Meghan, now engaged in tertiary studies, admitted:

> when we did that MASSIVE assignment this page was one of my first places to visit when the deadline loomed closer, nearly every different time I logged on there would be a handful of new questions by other students which were a huge help for me. It was extremely handy to be able to ask a teacher my probing questions regardless of whether it was 8am or 2am. It was also a great discussion starting point, meaning I could interact with my other history buddies about issues relating to the subject, a bit like having you all in my living room! I think it is definitely an advantage for a school subject to use the Facebook medium. It meant more support, more resources, and more discussion. Frankly, I miss it!

So this is another way to achieve that sought-after alchemy that engages students and encourages them to start thinking like historians.

The historical approach to primary sources, as outlined by Wineburg (2010), can be easily encouraged and extended using Facebook. Posting new content on the news feed can provide the basis of a discussion about the evidence contained in the source. Wineburg outlines several strategies that can be used via Facebook that will help students develop the skills of the historian and encourage them to recognise how a historian thinks. He argues that the first consideration is *sourcing*. Many students will find a source that they find difficult to interpret, and at Year 13 this will usually occur outside of class. Here the resulting discussion on Facebook can help others facing the same issue with different sources.

His next consideration is *contextualising*: the news feed is perfectly positioned to provide a context for the document concerned—possibly more so than the traditional classroom. Here you can place links to relevant sites, film clips and other sources that will help students start to place the document in its context, and the resulting discussion, guided by the teacher, will also help with this concept.

Wineburg's third key strategy is *close reading*, a skill now specified as an essential element in the external historical sources strand of the NCEA Achievement Standards. Using Facebook, teachers can encourage students to consider what the document is saying, what it is inferring, and the language that is being used. Again, discussion can be initiated with other students and the wider Facebook community.

Use of *background knowledge*, Wineburg's next strategy for teaching students how to think like a historian, can also be explored and shared on Facebook, as can his final strategy of *corroborating*. Facebook lends itself to this strategy perfectly. Here students can agree or disagree with ideas, post other sources to challenge underlying assumptions, or debate points of view, and all this can be seen on the news feed, encouraging others to join in.

What have I got out of this?

This experience has taught me that, in essence, students *want* to learn, to engage and to understand their world. I have been amazed at the responses I have had to the page and the maturity of my girls. (Yes, there are times when there is some joviality, and students love it when you show a sense of humour!) I have received queries about current television programmes, assessments, links, cartoons and websites, all outside of school hours and all on history. Why? Because they love the medium and have simply incorporated it into the way they network.

When it comes to the interactions on the page, I often can't respond instantly, but the girls know there will be a response within a few hours. Does this mean an increase in workload? Everyone I speak to has a different opinion, but in my experience and in my approach to teaching the answer is no. I am already using Facebook to keep an eye on my page and to see what my friends are up to throughout the country and overseas, so the *History at*

Queen's page gets checked as well. To me this is an investment, not work. It is a little bit of time invested in the learning of our young people, using their medium. Some nights I may spend an hour responding to queries, other nights there may be nothing, but regardless, it isn't *work*. It is helping to develop in my girls a love of learning and a passion for history. It is not something else to add to my workload—if anything it reduces it. I can sort out issues before they get too big; I can encourage the completion of tasks and clarify instructions, all long before someone decides "It's too hard" and gives up. As Malik (2012) claims, we need to treat Facebook as a "tool for real time interactions, thus saving us time yet keeping connected". The page itself becomes a growing resource: previous discussions are there to be shared. A number of these will re-run from year to year and task to task, so ongoing access to the debates that were held and the suggestions and decisions made can be seen as a positive trade-off in terms of workload: I don't have to repeat the process with each class.

The other major spin-off from this exercise is the relationship that you build with your students. No longer are you just a teacher in a class they pass through for a few hours a week. By having a page such as *History at Queen's,* you show you are interested in using their media and are approachable outside of teaching hours. It also underlines the teacher's role as learner as you share and contribute. The relationship you build is one of mutual respect and trust: they learn how to use the page responsibly with you setting the boundaries, and this transfers to the classroom. For many students the realisation that you are there to help and guide their learning outside of the usual 9 to 3 enhances the classroom relationship.

Further ideas

Facebook has a myriad of other uses, including being a potential medium for assessments. Achievement Standard 91004 *Demonstrate understanding of different perspectives of people in and historical event of significance to New Zealanders* is perfectly suited to using Facebook or a WordPress blog. Introduce some technology standards to sit under history and you start developing a course that will appeal to all sorts of kids. My Level 1 students started looking at perspectives through a task that had them developing a mini Facebook page, and then moving on to developing WordPress blogs for AS91004. This was a steep learning curve, but it has provided the girls with new ICT skills which are transferrable to other areas of their lives and schooling.

The task we devised was set in the Black Civil Rights context, where numerous perspectives can be explored. My students were asked to choose an event for which there were at least two perspectives that were clearly different and to start to explore how the people involved responded to the event. The beauty of blogs is that you can add in comments: one person sets up the blog and other people can comment on their perspective and actions, thus demonstrating perspectives in action. A word of caution: I have found that while Facebook allows this sort of interaction, it doesn't allow for the depth that is required for students to be able to achieve at Excellence level. However, it does provide a means of communication about the blog being developed and the ability of teacher and peers to challenge the ideas and assumptions being made by the blogger.

The other beauty of WordPress blogs, besides being free, is that you can make as many as you like, you can set them to 'private', and you can invite people to belong to your blog: no-one else needs to know about it or read it. Yes, there is some pre-teaching required in order to get students au fait with the programme—if they don't already know it—but this is minimal because the software is very easy to manoeuvre around and work with. Once my students had an understanding of the site and how to access their 'dashboard', they spent time working out which template suited them and then customised their blog by adding widgets and custom menus, photographs and videos (if they could find them), all adding depth to their perspectives and thus demonstrating a comprehensive understanding. Blogging is a very powerful social media tool, one that can be easily adapted for use by teachers as both a teaching tool and an assessment tool, and there are any number of examples in cyberspace where this is being done successfully. Some of the ones I enjoy reading include *History is Elementary*, *A Blast From the Past*, *History Today* and *The History Blog*, to name a few.

Facebook has the advantage of allowing those students who may not be comfortable asking questions in a classroom the opportunity to do so with impunity. It must be said, though, that Facebook does not replace face-to-face conversations and classroom mentoring: it complements the teaching process. Those classroom conversations and the direct work with students and documents are invaluable to students because they learn the craft of the historian in ways that cannot be replaced by Facebook. However, those questions you forget to ask at the time, and which come to you later, can be posted on the page to refocus and maintain students' engagement with the task. These second chances provide the capacity to extend, record and revisit the discussion in the classroom.

The social networking technology that is available to us as teachers has so many possibilities for engaging our students, developing relationships and developing a love of learning. To me, the obvious question is not why would you use it but why *wouldn't* you use it as a means of communication and engagement? I will continue to use Facebook, and while some classes are more interested in using it than others, all my students are members of the page and receive the notifications, and they can choose whether or not to respond.

References

Ayers, E. (1999). *The pasts and futures of digital history*. University of Virginia. Retrieved 23 January 2012 from http://www.vcdh.virginia.edu/PastsFutures.html

Childs, E. (2008). *Using Facebook as a teaching tool*. Retrieved 24 January 2012 from http://praxis.technorhetoric.net/index.php/Using_Facebook_as_a_Teaching_Tool

Couillard, C. (2010). *Facebook: The pros and cons of use in education*. Retrieved 27 January 2012 from http://clairecouillard.weebly.com/uploads/5/1/9/8/5198042/research_paper_tcs_701.pdf

Malik, O. (2012). *Why do we have Facebook fatigue?* Retrieved 28 January 2012 from http://gigaom.com/2007/07/29/facebook-fatigue/

Towner, T. L., VanHorn, A., & Parker, S. L. (2007). Facebook: Classroom tool for a classroom community? *Midwestern Political Science Association*, 1–18, as cited in http://clairecouillard.weebly.com/uploads/5/1/9/8/5198042/research_paper_tcs_701.pdf

Wineburg, S. (2010). Historical thinking: Memorising facts and stuff? *Teaching with Primary Sources*, *3*(1). Retrieved from http://www.loc.gov/teachers/tps/quarterly/historical_thinking/index.html

CHAPTER 8

Contestable views and voices: If only history involved time travel!

CHARLOTTE MCNAMARA

Charlotte McNamara has been a secondary school teacher in New Zealand for 8 years and is currently head of social sciences at Paraparaumu College. She has been involved in a lot of curriculum change in her current school and is enthusiastic about the changes in teaching and learning approaches and assessment in history. Charlotte is particularly interested in maintaining the relevance of learning history to students' lives. She is passionate about teaching and learning, and believes that publications such as this one provide wonderful opportunities for history educators to learn from each other and to develop a strong teaching community in the subject for the 21st century and beyond.

Charlotte can be contacted at: bec@paraparaumucollege.school.nz

Introduction

We can learn from history how past generations thought and acted, how they responded to the demands of their time and how they solved their problems. We can learn by analogy, not by example, for our circumstances will always be different than theirs were. The main thing history can teach us is that human actions have consequences and that certain choices, once made, cannot be undone. They foreclose the possibility of making other choices and thus they determine future events. (Gerda Lerner) I have been thinking a lot over the past few years about the way I teach history. This was prompted because I was working in my role as head of social studies/social sciences to implement the changes associated with the revised New Zealand curriculum. As I began to gain more of an understanding of second-order historical concepts, I realised how effective a history course with a strong focus on the concept of historical agency could be.

My teaching of history was previously through the lens of first-order concepts such as key personalities and events. However, I now believe that the traditional focus on content and the skill development it involves is not the best way to teach history. This shift in my thinking has enabled me and my students to see their learning of history as a *process* of understanding. We have explored more thoroughly the why and how of the decisions and actions of, and the consequences for, the individuals, groups and institutions that encompass historical events. My students have been able to interpret sources and evidence mindful of how they will go about gaining a more fruitful understanding of these people of the past.

I have had discussions with my colleagues about our various approaches to teaching about the people in history to the people of the present. We want our students to be able to interpret the people of the past as best they can, as people of *their* present. With a conceptual focus on individual, collective and institutional identity within Aotearoa/New Zealand framing our Year 9 social studies programme, and on worldviews in relation to human rights, social justice and environmental justice at Year 10, a connection to these concepts in senior history that incorporates historical agency seems logical as a key part of course design.

I have since been designing my senior history course to explicitly refer to and develop students' ability to process and understand information about people of the past through the lens of historical agency. My altered approach is still a work in progress, and so my main aim in this chapter is to examine this central concept of historical agency. I will explain some of the ways I have tried to get my students to gain a more meaningful understanding of people in the past, from the ordinary citizen to the revolutionary change-maker, seeing them as agents of their individual lives and circumstances. I encourage my students to do this wary of my own assumptions and stereotyping of small and large personalities of the past, and indeed of the interpretations contained in our textbook sources (Francis; Willinsky; Said; as cited in den Heyer, 2003).

I had often thought about the idea that as history teachers we are seldom prepared to acknowledge that what we deliver to our students is just *an* interpretation of the past. This is perhaps founded on the traditional notion that interpreting and packaging knowledge into digestible chunks is the primary purpose of teaching. In my earlier years of teaching I was more reluctant to admit that my version of the past could be challenged. However, in recent years, and influenced by my experiences in broader curriculum change, I have become more willing to acknowledge this with my students. I explain to them how I have come to my interpretation, share alternative interpretations with them, and then allow them learning opportunities to create their own version of the history we are examining. This approach does require some groundwork in terms of modelling for students how one might go about getting an interpretation of the agency of particular individuals, groups or institutions. This includes coverage of historical methods through whole-class, small-group and individual analysis of these agents within an historical context. I believe this empowers learners of history to engage in critical thinking and to become creators of knowledge for themselves and others, rather than being passive receivers of knowledge. Some students may not feel confident about the apron strings being loosened, and choose to simply accept my interpretation, but others relish the opportunity to come up with their own.

Our curriculum stipulates that learners of history in New Zealand should be challenged to engage with the past ethically, and with respect and integrity (Ministry of Education, 2007). I believe that a focus on historical agency goes a long way towards achieving this goal for our students.

Possible approaches to explore the concept of agency in history classrooms

First and foremost history is the study of people. Considering historical agency when learning history involves having an understanding of people as products of their times. Enabling our students to access these seemingly distant personalities—their motivations, decisions, actions, and the impact of these—in an attempt to construct their own meaning from the past is essential. Careful consideration of who we include from which contexts in our history curriculum is an important part of this (den Heyer, 2003). As history teachers we need to provide opportunities for our students to gain insight into and understanding of historical events through individual, collective and institutional historical agency and the subsequent outcomes of this agency in terms of whether or not situations in people's lives continued to stay the same or changed.

In order to get our students to recognise and understand the different types of historical agency, it is imperative that they are aware that different people experience historical events differently, and that "Groups and individuals [gain and] exercise power differently, depending on the social, cultural, economic, and political forces shaping the world in which they are acting" (Levstik, 2010). It is our role to provide learning activities that allow students to explore and understand this aspect of historical agency and the external and internal factors that influence individual, collective and institutional decision-making and action.

For example, in studying *The American Revolution and the Making of the Republic* and *Vietnam and the Conflict in Indochina*, my students have learnt about the historical forces and movements of nationalism, imperialism and revolution that are common to both. However, the long- and short-term causes, the motivations, decisions and actions of those involved, and the consequences related to influencing change, were considerably different. Equally important were the ways in which a strong sense of national identity free from the imperialism of foreign powers developed in each context. To personalise these forces in terms of the agents involved is important to our students' learning because it allows them to make comparisons and to contrast different events that we deem significant in the making of the modern world. It can also provide opportunities for students to relate to personalities of the past as agents in contemporary society (Seixas; Touraine; as cited in den Heyer, 2003).

To do this is relatively straightforward. One way is to provide students with a basic definition of these historical forces/movements and then provide them with material (historical evidence, both primary and secondary and in different mediums) to profile different individuals. This might include those in a position of power at the time, those who were affected by decisions that were made in the political sphere, and those who rebelled against the status quo. Students then have the tools to form their own version of the ways in which historical agents contributed to and were influenced by the forces surrounding them. This sort of activity allows students to develop a more objective and perceptive understanding of and appreciation for the people who create the changes that we tend to depersonalise as historical forces or movements. Students might like to communicate their understanding of these historical agents and their actions using the medium of the newspaper and writing editorials and letters to the editor, as well as writing press releases and interview transcripts.

Following Seixas (as cited in den Heyer, 2003), I believe it is also vital when studying a foreign context to bring the learning closer to home. Familiarity of context gives students a basis from which to explore the concept of historical agency in more depth. For example, in studying *Vietnam and the Conflict in Indochina*, we can provide resources and tasks to analyse and debate New Zealand's involvement in Vietnam with our students. This would uncover the divisions created within society at the time and after the event. Comparison of 'foreign' with more 'local' agents can only enhance students' understanding of the broad contexts encompassing this conflict. It may also lead to class discussions and debate, whereby students are asked to consider their own level of patriotism when asked, 'Would you volunteer to fight for your country if the time came?' In asking such questions of our students, another level of understanding of agency can be achieved.

This approach also allows students to further examine the impact these historical agents had on their own lives and the lives of others. This can lead to more challenging questions in relation to the 'what ifs' of history, to evaluate the impact an individual, a group or an institution had at the time, and after the time, they were active. Conducting activities with our students that give them the opportunity to isolate people, groups, institutions and events in history allows them to experiment with cause and consequence and predict various eventualities. We can then help them to make connections with this way of using and understanding information about 'significant' people in the past to form a coherent and more perceptive argument in the essay writing requirements of external assessments.

In examining ways to develop our students' understanding of agency and to think more critically, we should look in more detail at the ways in which we teach history. Arguably, a strong understanding of context is essential to students' understanding of historical agency (Foster, 2001). Something I have trialled with my Year 12 history students in our study of the Second Indochina War, for example, is a more thorough exploration of the life and times of the American presidents and their policies through analysing a range of sources and evidence. The aim is to encourage students to avoid presentism and challenge their own, and perhaps my, assumptions that tend to lean towards harsh criticism of the actions of successive American presidents in relation to their decisions regarding American involvement in Vietnam. We need to enable our students to explore the context and the very real fear of communism, and how that was grounded in the power struggle between the East and the West in the Cold War and the Korean War, as well as the fervent belief in the domino theory. While we may now see these as over-reaction to an unreal fear, we and our students should avoid using present world views to make judgements on the actions and decisions of people in the past. As Barton has said:

> Our natural sympathy [in a topic such as *Vietnam and the Conflict in Indochina* is] for the abuses people suffered, or for the constraints on their lives, can lead us to highlight what was done *to* them, rather than what they themselves did. (Barton, 2010)

In attempting to address this disparity, and the potential for others, I carried out the following activity. Students were given a model of an activity they were going to carry out in small groups. I did this through a comparison of the presidents Ho Chi Minh (North Vietnam) and Ngo Dinh Diem (South Vietnam). I started with a continuum on the whiteboard and asked students to consider which end of the continuum they would place Ho Chi Minh and Ngo Dinh Diem, from a very successful and effective leader at one end to a very unsuccessful and ineffective leader at the other. They also had to be prepared to justify why they put them there. As I had predicted, most students shared the same view/perception as I did: Ho Chi Minh was viewed more favourably than Ngo Dinh Diem. I then admitted to them that over my years of teaching this topic I had always promoted Ho Chi Minh as a somewhat flawless, inspirational leader. I then explained to them how I had challenged my own assumptions, based on research I had done around the topic prior to and while teaching it over the past 5 years. I explained that I had examined sources and discovered material that contradicted my original perception of Ho Chi Minh and his achievements. I then conducted the same exercise to challenge my more negative perception of Ngo Dinh Diem. I concluded my findings with a summary of key decisions and actions of each leader while president and the causes and consequences of these, as well as an overall evaluation of each of them.

There are many historical figures you could use for this exercise. It was successful in challenging my students to question my delivery of a topic and their own interpretations and assumptions about significant people. It also allowed greater exploration of the factors related to historical agency, including, context, experiences, motivations and beliefs that caused these agents to develop identities that had both positive and negative impacts on the institutions and people they led.

Students then worked in small groups to evaluate the successes and failures resulting from American presidents' decisions and actions regarding American involvement in Vietnam. It may be true that:

> Power is a familiar concept to students who, with relatively little prompting, understand not only that larger forces may limit or expand opportunities for action, but that individuals may not all respond in the same way to those opportunities (Levstik, 2010).

However, further inquiry into this concept allows greater understanding of the agency of political leaders. My students were challenged to research each president in small groups and consider the long- and short-term causes (considering context and historical forces) of decisions they made and actions they took. They then had to prioritise the key decisions/actions and summarise the short- and long-term consequences of these. In order to prepare a presentation for the rest of the class, they also wrote a final evaluation of that president's leadership with regard to American involvement in Vietnam. Students delivered oral presentations of their findings and some even considered using their research as the foundation material for an externally assessed essay, using the president as a 'significant' identity. This activity allowed my students to see these leaders more as people, as agents, and perhaps even as victims of the times in which they lived. I believe it allowed them to interpret these people more authentically and to develop a more balanced view of them.

An important way to support our students in their ability to understand and appreciate historical agency it is to raise the question 'How do we know what we know about the past?' In attempting to explore this with my Year 12 history students, I undertook an activity related to our study of the First Indochina War and the significance of the Battle of Dien Bien Phu. I began the lesson with the question 'How can we ever really know the truth about what happened to the people on each side of the Battle of Dien Bien Phu?' I allowed them some time to read and process the question and prompted students to discuss with their peers ways in which we can obtain an understanding as close as possible to the truth. In doing so, students were able to draw on their own previous experience with assessment tasks involving the inquiry process. This included questioning, resource interpretation, and source and evidence evaluation skills. Students' tactics included using a range of sources, comparing and contrasting different sources and evidence, viewing evidence with a critical eye, using primary evidence (although a tendency for students to assume that evidence from the time must be more 'true' is problematic), and exploring multiple perspectives.

Students were then asked to consider as part of their inquiry aspects such as authorship. Examining valuable primary resources to consider the possible conscious and unconscious purposes, values and world view of authors provides another angle from which we can analyse historical agency with students. I also suggested that students analyse a source and evidence in view of its historical background and its historical setting. These approaches led some students to feel a little uneasy about historical knowledge. It is this uneasiness that we want to foster, or rather encourage students to have, to develop informed, critical thinking through which they view information within and well beyond our history classrooms.

Another example of this was when we were examining the topic *The American Revolution and the Making of the Republic*, whereby each significant event in this topic was also explored through exposing students to a wide range of sources and evidence. As the students were learning about events, they were encouraged to critically analyse information created at and after the event in a variety of formats. They had to make decisions to explain how useful that evidence was in helping the development of their understanding of historical agency through interpretations and cause and effect. Some examples include Paul Revere's engravings compared and contrasted to the John Adams documentary series, the primary accounts of the Boston Massacre, and the Boston Massacre trial and its outcomes, as well as secondary historical articles about the contemporary bias and propaganda surrounding the event. The need to interpret evidence effectively to understand historical agency is largely based on our need to explore the

> values, attitudes, and beliefs of people in the past ... If we think that everyone in the past reasoned the way we do, then we may find ourselves holding them accountable to standards that they did not share. (Barton, 2010)

In order to further explore the concept of historical agency, rather than focus on the concept of cause and effect in the traditional sense, I have been trialling the use of perspectives causation and involvement in an event, as well as evaluating the success/failure of decisions and actions of the individuals/groups involved as consequences. For example, in teaching *The American Revolution and the Making of the Republic*, each 'significant event' covered was explored through the perspectives 'British reasons for ...', 'Colonists responses to ...', as well as the key features of the event itself. This approach enables greater exploration of the concept of historical agency, and provides a better opportunity for our students to develop an understanding of "What [decision] and action was possible [or not possible] given the historical moment" to allow them to make sense of past behaviours (Levstik, 2010). It encourages less generalising of historical agents because students are shown how to distinguish agents from each other when analysing social change. For example, rather than using the term 'colonists' to unify the experiences of those involved in the American

Revolution, students are encouraged to consider these agents of change or continuity under a more historically accurate grouping, such as the Sons of Liberty or Loyalists (den Heyer, 2003).

In my and my colleagues' experiences as teachers of Year 11, 12 and Year 13 history, 'understanding historical perspectives' has always been an area where students struggle to gain the higher grades in comparison to the other NCEA Achievement Standard tasks. Despite scaffolding students through steps in relation to their planning of ideas and modelling the format required in the task, results still do not appear to indicate that students are grasping it as well as we would hope. In Year 13 history and the study of Tudor–Stuart England, the perspectives are not specifically examined, although they are an integral part of students' ability to understand the time period and the monarchs well enough to write essays related to them as leaders.

In order to empower our students with the confidence and capability to explain historical perspectives, and indeed agency (such as reasons for opinions, decisions and actions, and responses to others' opinions, decisions and actions and why there was that specific response), we need to create appropriate learning tasks. These tasks need to connect the significant identities to the social, cultural, political, economic and environmental contexts which they were born into and influenced by. We would not be preparing our students adequately if we were to simply ask them to 'relate to' or 'put themselves in the shoes of' people in the past. Thoroughly outlining events in context and the agents involved is essential to students forming justified explanations. They will then be able to reveal their understanding of historical agency more effectively in a specific assessment task situation.

Another way in which agency can be explored is through research questions and challenging historiography that show the ways in which certain individuals and groups have been portrayed as having more or less agency than others; for example, the oppressors versus the oppressed. Students should be encouraged to ask questions about what actions people took and why, and what external influences either supported or restrained them in the process. Using such questions in research-based assessment tasks will lead students to use a wider variety of evidence to discover their own interpretation and to evaluate the level of agency displayed by individuals, groups and institutions.

Apart from the way in which we prepare students for assessment tasks at Years 11, 12 and 13 by focusing more specifically on the concept of historical agency, we can also develop our students' understanding of this concept by carefully structuring the course, or by the way we teach it. For example, in the Tudor–Stuart England topic in Year 13, I believe perspectives are more related to historical agency in terms of personal monarchy. Using this approach to teaching this course means that students are able to analyse and evaluate the decisions and actions of each monarch within the complex context of their family lives, the numerous, political, economic and social issues they contended with, and the legacies they left. As with any leader, past or present, to be fair to them in their position of responsibility, we need to fully explore the circumstances in which they ruled and consider the prevailing culture. In doing so, we cover both the intrinsically and extrinsically motivated decisions and actions of these historical agents.

The time is right for change

Given that our curriculum is currently undergoing realignment, now is the time to carefully consider *how* we are going to develop key historical thinking and key understandings of historical concepts, and the *what*, the *who* and the *ways* in which we teach history. I have been arguing that we should start with the people and delve into the multiple layers of their lives to determine what factors influenced their decisions and actions, their responses and reactions, their successes and failures. This is where a concept-based approach based on people as opposed to key historical events would be ideal. Crossing time periods and places to explore the realities of existence for people then and now encourages our students to engage and to see the relevance of history. It also allows them to grow as lifelong learners and develop their personalities from a base of historical understanding.

Affirming the relevance of history also requires us to be conscious of our responsibility to emphasise the ethical nature of our subject.

> Making moral judgements depends on knowing who was responsible for an action; we can assign praise or blame only if we can identify the agent ... Although some historians, and some history educators denounce moral judgements in the teaching and learning of history, morality is central to the way most people make sense of the past. (Barton, 2010)

It is imperative that we, as teachers, provide our students with a balanced and authentic representation of the people of the past to avoid making judgements on their decisions and actions from our own moral understanding of the present. Emphasising the need to be aware of this relates to our role in supporting our students to adopt a more objective approach to historical material, while at the same time developing their own character and conscience from a variety of past, present and future contexts.

This rationale in terms of why a teaching and learning approach in history based on agency is effective can be coupled with the need to avoid the problems associated with students acting or not acting as historians. What we do need to consider are our genuine aims for our students beyond our classrooms and within the wider discipline of history. I was recently reminded of this after a student of mine was interviewed and could not explain to the interviewer the point of studying or learning history. This made me realise that I had not adequately contemplated the need to invite my students to see the wider relevance of history. I needed to facilitate my students' ability to learn history through historical thinking concepts in order to gain a real sense of the discipline of history and its purpose beyond the classroom.

Increasingly our students are questioning the relevance of learning specific subjects, given that knowledge is so accessible in many different formats. We need to provide opportunities and have explanations at the ready to assure them that the study of history and its people spans time and place. Ultimately, it allows us as individuals at any given moment in time to be amazed, influenced, appreciative or disheartened at the decisions and actions of others. We want these emotional reactions to trigger a response and a feeling of relatable understanding for students in their own lives, at any given time, in any given place then, now, or in the future.

Conclusion

A framework for teaching and learning history based on the concept of historical agency can be very effective. It provides opportunities for our students to think critically about historical information in their quest to reach out to the people of the past. Students can then piece together and analyse all the parts of the complex existence of these people in history much more genuinely. It allows our students to gain a much richer view of the world and their place in it. This in turn highlights the value of history as a subject that influences our students as they grow and decide the kind of individual they want to be in these complex times. A focus on historical agency is vitally important in relation to the personal agency we want our students to develop. After all,

> agency is at the heart of the public sphere. To participate in the public life of democracy is to think, to judge, and to act—and all these depend on a concept of oneself and others as individuals who make choices about desired social ends, who decide how to pursue goals, and who are both enabled and constrained in doing so by the wider world. (Barton, 2010)

If we can foster this in our students, more of them will be able to confidently justify in their own words why history matters to *them*.

References

Barton, K. (2010). Agency overview. Unpublished manuscript. University of Indiana, Bloomington, IN.

Den Heyer, K. (2003). Between every 'now' and 'then': A role for the study of historical agency in history and citizenship education. *Theory and Research in Social Education, 31*(4), 411-434.

Foster,S.J. (2001). Historical empathy in theory and practice: Some final thoughts. In O. L. Davis Jr, E. A. Yeager, & S. J. Foster (Eds.), *Historical empathy and perspective taking in the social studies* (pp. 167-181). Lanham, MD: Rowman & Littlefield Publishers.

Lerner, G. (n.d.). *Gerder Lerner quotes. Quotes n Sayings*. Retrieved 25 August 2011 from http://www.quotesnsayings.net/quotes/12313

Levstik,L. (2010). *Historical agency in history book sets*. Retrieved 25 August 2011 from http://teachinghistory.org/teaching-materials/teaching-guides/22365

Ministry of Education.(2007). The New Zealand curriculum. Wellington: Learning Media.

CHAPTER 9

Where to next? Some final thoughts on the future of history teaching in New Zealand

MICHAEL HARCOURT

> Michael Harcourt has been teaching history and social studies for 7 years and is currently teaching at Wellington High School. He is interested in developing spatial approaches to the past and looking at how the local environment can be used to develop students' enthusiasm for learning history. He is also interested in the ways that students' ideas about the past are shaped by their socio-cultural backgrounds, and how teachers can use this information to inform their teaching. He has recently been investigating how to incorporate digital tools into his classroom practices and is particularly inspired by historians such as Geoff Park, Rachel Buchanan and Howard Zinn.
>
> Michael can be contacted at michael.harcourt@whs.school.nz

Two key commemorative occasions over the next decade will result in the past playing a large role in the public's consciousness. The first, international in scope, begins in 2014 when 100 years since the outbreak of World War I will be marked. The high point in this part of the world will certainly be in 2015, as New Zealanders commemorate the anniversary of the Gallipoli campaign. These commemorative activities will culminate on 11 November 2018 with the anniversary of the war's end. The second commemorative occasion will take place in 2019 as New Zealanders, Australians and other Pacific peoples mark 250 years since James Cook's first voyage. With these anniversaries we can expect a multimedia bonanza of documentaries, books, exhibition displays, websites, iPad applications, curriculum resources and commentary from politicians, academics, journalists and bloggers.

These commemorations demand a thoughtful response from history teachers. Historical events such as war and 'discovery' can become uniquely exclusivist, celebratory narratives, more to do with mobilising national identity than with explaining the past. Peter Seixas argues that

> the memory of war is the gold standard as an instrument to shore up the coherence of the national story, the valourizing of national heroes, and the significance of the nation on the national stage. (2009, p. 19)

Elsewhere Seixas has described celebratory teaching of the past as a "best story approach", which "at best [comes] in the form of gripping and vivid stories with a moral trajectory; at worst, it is a desiccated version of the past, a relatively meaningless batch of names, dates, and events" (2000, p.23). Others draw distinctions between "history" and "heritage", or "disciplinary history" and "memory history". The former terms reflect the conceptual tools and dispositions unique to the structure of the discipline and the practice of historians, whereas the latter involve "an unscientific study of history, subject to the dialectic of remembering and forgetting" (Levesque, 2008, pp. 6–7). Levesque argues that disciplinary thinking "offer[s] people formidable 'ways of knowing' about past or current issues of significance" (2008, p. 7).

Over the past 5 years the New Zealand history teaching community has become increasingly focused on disciplinary ways of knowing, or what is commonly called historical thinking or 'historical literacy'. The teachers and educators in this book all show different possibilities for how teachers can systematically put historical thinking into classroom practices. Such practices are not an abdication of teachers' responsibility to develop content knowledge, because information and facts about historical events should be taught in ways that develop historical thinking. Learning theorist James Gee argues that "if you want to design a learning environment, don't start with the content" (2004, p. 118). Dismissing what he terms the "content fetish", Gee suggests teachers start with questions such as "What experiences do I want learners to have? What do I want them to be able to do?" (2004, p. 118).

The work done by the teachers in this book (and many other likeminded ones around the country) needs to be built upon so that all students who choose to study history are consistently learning how to actively judge and debate historical significance, evaluate historical causation, assess historical agency, interpret historical evidence, question historical interpretations and recognise historical perspectives without making presentist assumptions. Students (and their teachers) need to be deeply familiar with the idea that historical knowledge is always tentative and contested, and that this knowledge is produced and legitimised within a disciplinary framework (Mojo, 2008, p. 103). Put another way, in addition to students *learning* historical narratives, they also need to *make* historical narratives as well as "[understand] how those narrative[s] are made" (Chapman, et al, 2011, p. 22). This book marks only the beginning of a much-needed public conversation that offers alternatives to the nationalist, best-story approach to history teaching described by Seixas.

It may be easier to fall into the trap of teaching a nationalist history than many teachers realise. The *New Oxford History of New Zealand* (Byrnes, 2009) exposes deep assumptions about the direction and purpose of New Zealand history. Two dominant themes evident in representations of New Zealand's past are acknowledged in this book as highly problematic. The first is the manner in which New Zealand history is often explained as a "quest for national identity" (p. 1). Based on ideas of progressive and evolutionary development, these historical narratives start from a Polynesian homeland, move to a colonial outpost, and culminate in an independent nation state (p. 1). The editor, Giselle Byrnes, argues that such narratives serve as "colonising practices". She draws on the work of New Zealand cultural historian Peter Gibbons, who writes:

> Those histories which propose national identity/nationhood/nationalism as the normative narrative, which consider national identity to be a natural, even organic growth rather than an ideological construction, and which conceal how national identity is fabricated within the

broader processes of colonization, are themselves colonising texts, not 'representations' of the past but *practices* with real and continuing consequences. (2002, p. 14) (Emphasis in original.)

The second dominant theme that Byrnes challenges is the tendency to consider New Zealand history as unique, distinct and exceptional. She suggests, instead, that New Zealand history is better served by a *transnational* approach, which acknowledges the ways in which culture, political activity, economic and social trends are "part of a much larger canvas" (2009, p. 1).

What does this mean for secondary school history teachers? In defining a "nationalist interpretation of New Zealand history" Byrnes offers some useful descriptors that serve as a valuable starting point for discussion (see Table 9.1).

Table 9.1. Nationalist interpretations of New Zealand history

Do:	Do not:
Assume the central status of "the 'colony-to-nation' narrative"	"take into account the diversity of lived historical experiences"
"eclipse the degree to which New Zealand had contact with other places"	"problematise Pākehā historical experiences, but instead consider them as normal, natural and innate"
"[obscure] the extent to which the lives of New Zealanders have been affected by international as well as domestic trends"	Pay enough attention to "plurality and difference"
"Exclude other narratives and alternative histories"	

Source: Byrnes, 2009, p. 7

One way that history teachers might begin to respond to these new directions in New Zealand historiography is to use the points above when considering how to emplot New Zealand's past with students. Simone Schweber illustrates the concept of emplotment in her research on how several history teachers represented the Holocaust to American students.

She shows how teachers unwittingly individualised or collectivised, normalised or exoticised, personalised or abstracted Jewish experiences of the Holocaust. She also shows the extent to which teachers represented history as "infused by individual decisions rather than dictated by larger societal forces" (2004, p. 157). Schweber concludes by suggesting three questions teachers should always explicitly consider: "What emplotment makes sense for this historical event or episode, and why? How ought the various groups of historical actors involved be represented? How am I representing history itself?" (2004, p. 158). As the arguments in *The New Oxford History of New Zealand* filter through the history teaching community, Schweber's questions serve as a useful heuristic to consider how the 'text' of teaching practices might need to be reconsidered.

Teachers who uncover the frameworks their students use to make sense of the past are in a much better position to respond to this knowledge in ways that widen understanding and increase capacity for thoughtful, civic participation. In the United States, the effects of students relying on a nationalist framework for understanding the past have been comprehensively described and challenged by educationalists (Epstein, 2009; Levstik, 2000). Linda Levstik researched American students' and teachers' conceptions of historical significance and found there was a considerable tendency to leave uncomfortable pasts out of the national narrative. She argues that

> in societies in which contemporary groups experience wide differences in their economic or social status, the emancipatory historical stories serve to establish the legitimacy of the status quo and dissipate concern about the persistence of disparities in circumstance. (p. 290)

Levstik offers three questions for historical inquiry that she believes may help history teachers to challenge these disparities: "What constituencies have various social, political, and economic systems apparently served? To what uses have these systems been put by various empowered and disempowered agents? Which ethnoracial categories have been introduced when and by whom, and who, if anyone, resisted their application and in what context?" (2000, p. 299). Levstik's analysis of students' and teachers' frameworks for understanding American history poses some interesting 'teaching as inquiry' challenges for teachers in this country to explore in their classrooms.

In New Zealand, a consequence of teaching a nationalist best story is that Māori histories are silenced (Buchanan, 2011, p. 285). Indeed, the history teaching profession has recently been criticised for not adequately representing Māori (Sharples, 2010). Teachers have been accused of "sidestepping" and "avoiding" certain topics due to their controversial nature ("Call to stop teachers 'avoiding' Maori history", 2010, p. A7). Other New Zealand studies have found that controversial issues in the social sciences are avoided (Keown, Harrison 1998). In my experience, contentious events (especially ones related to the European colonisation of New Zealand) can sometimes inspire heated classroom discussion and erroneous thinking based on deeply engrained prejudice. The thought of unleashing an emotional response that confirms beliefs not informed by careful historical thinking creates a certain desire to avoid issues and historical events that students may find difficult, or may not want to learn about at all.

However, it is also my experience that, through thinking historically, students can learn to apply reasoned judgement after careful analysis of the evidence. They are then able to participate in a discussion about the past and its relationship to the present and future much more constructively. For example, students who investigate a question such as, 'How has the government response to Māori assertions of their tino rangatiratanga changed over time?' are more likely to view (and be able to discuss) contemporary events, such as the October 2007 'anti-terror raids' in the Urewera, with a critical historical perspective. The new focus in the New Zealand curriculum on contested events is, therefore, particularly welcome, and a good opportunity for teachers to embrace the teaching of topics relating to the history and legacy of European colonisation and race relations.

This book demonstrates that learning to think historically has significant benefits for students. However, recently I was speaking to a Māori academic about different ways of understanding the past. She expressed concern that differentiating between memory history and disciplinary history (as described earlier) could be problematic because Māori and indigenous histories are likely to be placed in the inferior memory category. This is an important concern. If disciplinary thinking is used to undermine indigenous ways of thinking about the past, we are in real danger of what some have termed "cognitive imperialism", or using a Eurocentric framework for legitimating whose knowledge counts and whose does not (Reilly, 2011, p. xxv). Furthermore, educationalist Linda Tuhiwai Smith argues powerfully that "the negation of indigenous views of history was a critical part of asserting colonial ideology, partly because such views were regarded as clearly 'primitive' and 'incorrect' and mostly because they challenged and resisted the mission of colonization" (1999, p. 29). To avoid unconsciously undermining Māori histories, we can start by developing a critical attitude to the discipline of history. This is one of the major challenges for our profession.

Finally, the teachers and educators in this book have all shown, through their writing, a commitment and dedication to their students and history education that bodes well for the future. A former teacher of mine writes that

> one of the keys to a revival of education's spirit is the reclaiming of public education space. This is the space in which diverse education creeds are made to bump into each other in thoughtful exchanges and vigorous debate. (Neyland, 2010, p. xvi)

This book makes a contribution to these collisions of ideas, the energy from which will hopefully extend beyond its pages.

References

Buchanan, R. (2011). Re-making memory on Matiu and other 'settlement' sites. *Memory Connection, 1*(1), 284-300.

Byrnes, G. (2009). Introduction: Reframing New Zealand history. In G. Byrnes (Ed.), *The new Oxford history of New Zealand* (pp. 1-18). Melbourne, VIC: Oxford University Press.

Call to stop teachers 'avoiding' Maori history. (2010, 24 June). *The Dominion Post*, p. A7.

Chapman, A., Burn, K., Counsell, C., Fordham, M. (Eds.). (2011). Debates: Narrative in school history. *Teaching History*, 145, 22-31.

Epstein, T. (2009). *Interpreting national history: Race, identity, and pedagogy in classrooms and communities*. New York, NY: Routledge.

Gee, J. P. (2004). *Situated language and learning: A critique of traditional schooling*. New York, NY: Routledge.

Gibbons, P. (2002). Cultural colonization and national identity. *New Zealand Journal of History, 36*, 5-17.

Harrison, K. (1998). Social studies in the New Zealand curriculum: Dosing for amnesia or enemy of ethnocentricism? In P. Benson & R. Openshaw (Eds.), *New horizons for New Zealand social studies* (pp. 63-82). Palmerston North: ERDC Press.

Keown, P. (1998). Values and social action: Doing the hard bits. In P. Benson & R. Openshaw (Eds.), *New horizons for New Zealand social studies* (pp. 137-159). Palmerston North: ERDC Press.

Levesque, S. (2008). *Thinking historically: Educating students for the twenty-first century*. Toronto, ON: University of Toronto Press.

Levstik, L. (2000). Articulating the silences: Teachers' and adolescents' conceptions of historical significance. In P. Stearns, P. Seixas, & S. Wineburg (Eds.), *Knowing, teaching & learning history: National and international perspectives* (pp. 284-305). New York, NY: New York University Press.

Mojo, E. B. (2008). Foregrounding the disciplines in secondary literacy teaching and learning: A call for change. *Journal of Adolescent & Adult Literacy*, October, 96–107.

Neyland, J. (2010). *Rediscovering the spirit of education after scientific management*. Rotterdam, The Netherlands: Sense Publishers.

Reilly, C. (2011). Cognitive imperialism and decolonizing research: Modes of transformation. In C. Reilly, V. Russell, L. K. Chehayl, & M. M. McDermott (Eds.), *Surveying borders, boundaries, and contested spaces in curriculum and pedagogy* (pp. xv-xxviii). Charlotte: N.C, Information Age Publishing.

Schweber, S. (2004). *Making sense of the Holocaust*. New York, NY: Teachers College Press.

Seixas, P. (2000). Schweigen! Die Kinder! Or, does postmodern history have a place in the schools? In P. Stearns, P. Seixas, & S. Wineburg (Eds.), *Knowing, teaching & learning history: National and international perspectives* (pp. 19-37). New York, NY: New York University Press.

Seixas, P. (2009). National history and beyond. *Journal of Curriculum Studies, 41*(6), 719-722.

Sharples, P. (2010). Opening address to the New Zealand History Teachers' Association Conference, 4 October 2010. Retrieved 16 January 2012 from http://www.beehive.govt.nz/speech/new-zealand-history-teachers039-association-conference

Smith, L. T. (1999). *Decolonizing methodologies: Research and indigenous peoples*. Dunedin: University of Otago Press.

OPENING SPEECH

New Zealand History Teachers' Association
Conference, Wellington, 4 October 2010

Associate Minister of Education
The Right Honourable Dr Pita Sharples,
Co-leader Māori Party

This conference is all about challenging you to think about teaching different types of history in new ways. I would like to present a vision of this today. Why is it so difficult to explain to many New Zealanders the concepts of mana whenua and iwi taketake? Why do many New Zealanders regard the Treaty settlements process as a gravy train—even when the average value of settlements is about 1 percent of the value of the land lost? Why are New Zealanders not taught about the nature of those tools of colonisation which, in early New Zealand, were the absolute cause of the loss and near extinction of the Māori language—and I refer to the Tohunga Suppression Act; the role of the early Pākehā village school master and his family in determining the rights, and wrongs, of appropriate village behaviour; the deliberate practice of corporal punishment for speaking te reo Māori in the school grounds; and the associated negative stigma that these practices placed upon te reo Māori as a relevant and appropriate language for these islands?

DR PITA SHARPLES

Who was Huikai, and why was he famous? What role has our selective portrayal of New Zealand history played in shaping attitudes towards Māori–Pākehā relations, and contributed to many of the negative stereotypes that arise from time to time between the two peoples? Why has New Zealand history teaching failed to represent the indigenous people of these islands within their own distinctive cultural and spiritual values, which still today underpin the Māori genre de vie? Have the various presentations of our history, particularly over the past century, contributed in any way towards the promotion of Māori as negative? As second-class? As not as sophisticated in the ways of living as Pākehā are?

In my maiden speech in Parliament I addressed some of these questions. It is common knowledge that Māori do not enjoy the same socioeconomic and educational benefits as non-Māori in this, their country of origin. Yet it strikes me as somewhat amazing that half the country, and probably some of us here today, actually believe that Māori are the privileged group in our society. Cries of racial funding, gravy trains and special courses are constant within our society, and are eagerly published by every arm of the media to promote a negative stereotype of Māori.

If Māori are the privileged group, why, in my electorate, are Māori not living in prime locations like Kohimārama, St Heliers and Mission Bay? Conversely, why are they clustered in state housing sectors inland? Does privilege mean that we Māori dominate certain illnesses such as diabetes, heart disease, asthma, glue ear, and others, and that we die 10 years earlier than Pākehā? Or is our real privilege to be revealed in this country's disgusting incarceration figures? I say "disgusting" because in 1980 one in 1,000 New Zealanders was in jail, and in the early 1990s one in 800 was in jail. Five years ago one in 570 New Zealanders was in jail, but for Māori, the privileged group, one person in 180 was in jail.

So I ask this gathering: Why are Māori being promoted so negatively by politicians, the media, and, consequently, by non-thinking redneck New Zealanders? How can that be good for our future as a nation? When I was at school, it was said of our history lessons that New Zealanders learned a little about a lot, in contrast to students in the United States, who learned a lot about a little. We learn about the events of world history and about the cultural origins of countries' customs. Where is the recognition of the 1,500-year bond between Māori and these islands? Why do we accept the world's history and not our own?

The Spanish Inquisition, the French Revolution, the Battle of Waterloo, Plato, Aristotle, Socrates—we know about all these things; we know about those people. So what of Toi Kairākau, of Rauru? What of my history, my tangata whenua-ness, my 1,500 missing years?

Toi Kairākau crossed the Pacific and came to New Zealand. At the same time, Eric the Red was expelled from Iceland and voyaged to Greenland. Toi Kairākau is my ancestor; he still lives, in me. His history and genealogy are my history and genealogy, my bonding to these islands of Aotearoa. Toi's son was Rauru; his son was Whātonga. From Whātonga came Tahaiti; from Tahaiti came Uenuku. At the time of Uenuku, William of Normandy conquered England and became King William I. From Uenuku came Ruatapu; from Ruatapu came Rākeiora; from Rākeiora came Tama ki Te Hau. Those are my ancestors—tangata whenua—and the ancestor Tama ki Te Hau lived at the time of the great military leader Genghis Khan, who established the Mongol empire, uniting almost all of Asia and Europe.

My genealogy descends to Tama ki Te Rā and Tame ki Te Mātangi—and now the Magna Carta is signed on the other side of the world. I continue my whakapapa by naming Tama ki Reireia, Te Kāhuārero, Pito, Rere, Tangi, Maika, Toto, and Tamatea Arikinui. Tamatea Arikinui brought the tapu canoe of Tākitimu across the Pacific. He is the eponymous ancestor of all descendants of the Tākitimu waka and I descend from him. At this time, history records the crusade of Joan of Arc of France, who was burnt at the stake aged 19 years. From Tamatea Arikinui came Rongokākō; from Rongokākō came Tamatea Pōkai Whenua. His son was Kahungunu. Kahungunu was the founding ancestor of my tribe, Ngāti Kahungunu. Then came Kahukuranui, Rākaihikuroa, and Taraia. Taraia led the migration of my people, Kahungunu, from Wairoa south to the Napier–Hastings area. That is my history. At the same time Columbus stumbled upon America.

I move on from Taraia to Te Rangi-Taumaha to Te Huhuti. Te Huhuti married Te Whātuiāpiti. He was a great war chief. He had red hair. Those are the eponymous ancestors of our subtribe, Ngāti Te Whātuiāpiti. And

I lived in them, and now they live in me. Then came Te Wawahanga, Rangikawhiua, Te Manawakawa, and Te Rangikōianake, and at that time Cromwell overthrew the British monarchy and declared a republic. All that is history. Te Rangikōianake is the ancestor of the subtribe Ngāti Rangikōianake of Te Haukē. Also my grandson carries his name and his spirit. His eldest son was Te Kikiri o te Rangi, another chief—another famous war chief, another redhead. He led many successful forays to avenge the deaths of his two grandfathers. He is the eponymous ancestor of my subtribe, Ngāi Te Kikiri o te Rangi.

And the genealogy continues: his daughter was Kanohi Tū Hanga, who married Te Umurangi, famously recorded in the oriori *Pinepine te Kura*, to Te Aroatua, Hōri Niania, and Paora Kōpūkau Niania. He was my grandfather, and his name and his spirit are carried by my son, in whom I also live. From Paora came my mother, Ruihā, and then me. This is my history. This is tangata whenua, and this is New Zealand, history. This is our history. This genealogy is alive, with the people and the history of this place—a history untold. And there are 600,000 such genealogies existing within the Māori oral culture of today, of events and people of this place.

I have chosen to use this time to explain the importance of the concept of tangata whenua. I do so because I believe that the future of New Zealand is deeply intertwined with the future of Māoridom, and is, in the eyes of the global community, uniquely intertwined with the idea of this nation. In a world increasingly homogenised by global commerce, migration, communications, travel and trade, Māoridom provides an enduring point of difference that other cultures envy—a difference we must preserve.

For this nation to thrive economically, culturally, and with a sense of social justice, Māori must be able to play a full role in all parts of society, not only as leaders, educators, artists, business chiefs and sporting champions, but as citizens whose rights, culture and fundamental worth are valued and supported.

Although Māori have made great strides within kaupapa Māori initiatives, the reality of equality for Māori is still far off. So, then, how will we write our future? How will we write the history of the 2004 Foreshore and Seabed Act of Parliament? The entire country was led to believe that such a law was appropriate and fair but the decision to legislate was made by a few people, without consulting with the Māori Ministers and Māori members of the Government. Their opinions were not sought until after the decision to legislate had been made.

Second, the legislation produced the single greatest act of confiscation to date, and that occurred during the time of the Treaty settlements: "Wā-ā, ko te Kāwanatanga wā tā ringa ka-tau utua raupatu, Wā-ā tā ringa ma-auī tāhae taku tai moana—e!" (The right hand pays out for last century's confiscations, but the left hand steals more land.)

Third, public support for that legislation was sought by promoting the idea that Māori would stop public access to the beaches and, furthermore, might sell the asset offshore. I would like to remind us here that Māori culture is inclusive and not exclusive; for example, Māori leaders who represented a population of more than 100,000 signed a contract at Waitangi on 6 February 1840 with a people numbering only 2,000. It invited people not only to access and emigrate to our islands but to establish a government as well—surely a generous and an inclusive offer. Then, to add insult to insult, the Government used its Māori MPs to sell that Foreshore and Seabed Bill to the people. The final act of the Government was to disregard the United Nations report condemning the legislation as racist.

Does your historical representation of the 2004 Foreshore and Seabed Act coincide with my version? Will my version be taught as History 101? I want you to understand that the hurt to my people in that matter was very, very deep. To be regarded as not worthy of a voice, to be called "haters and wreckers", and to be held in contempt and ridicule cut even deeper than the legislation itself. That absolute disregard for Māori, for our views, for our customs, and for our mana, will not—*will not*—be allowed to happen again. Well, we've moved on, we're heading for repeal, and the replacement Bill has had its first reading in Parliament. Hopefully this episode from our recent history will enable us to reflect more wisely on earlier episodes of history, and will lead us to a different, more positive future.

Kia ora.

(Reproduced with permission from Dr Pita Sharples)

www.ingramcontent.com/pod-product-compliance
Lightning Source LLC
Chambersburg PA
CBHW081331230426
43667CB00018B/2901